ENTREPRENEURSHIP
—AND—
CULTURE

The Role of National Culture
in Entrepreneurship:
A Study of 51 Countries

Faisal Al-Kadi

ISBN: 978-1-4834-6359-9 (sc)
ISBN: 978-1-4834-6360-5 (hc)
ISBN: 978-1-4834-6358-2 (e)

Lulu Publishing Services rev. date: 01/24/2017

Originally a dissertation for a Doctorate in Business Administration (DBA) from IE Business School – Madrid, Spain. Advised by Dr. Cristina Cruz, the dissertation was unanimously approved by the Doctoral Committee with no reservation in May 2013.

CONTENTS

ABSTRACT

This dissertation proposes a theoretical justification and runs an empirical assessment of the national culture's influence on the systematic variation of aggregate entrepreneurship levels across nations. National culture, this study suggests, plays an instrumental role (positive/negative) in shaping the appetite of nations towards the acceptance and sustainability of entrepreneurial ventures. Seven cultural dimensions are studied at the country-level through a sample of 51 countries across 8 years; representing one of the largest samples in cross-country studies of this field. The study offers: an integrative approach that links culture to entrepreneurship, new associations, rationalizations of previous contradictory findings, assessment of popular measures, and a never-more-relevant topic and recommendations to today's turbulent global economy and changing country-competitiveness realities.

Main findings: The cultural dimension of Uncertainty Avoidance provides a negative impact on entrepreneurship levels; while Power Distance provides a positive impact. Collectivism was tested to have two contrasting influences on entrepreneurship levels; Institutional Collectivism being negative and In-Group Collectivism being positive. Future Orientation, contrary to expected, had a negative impact. Further analysis was also carried out by splitting countries into two groups based on income; revealing that the cultural dimensions of Performance Orientation and Assertiveness have a positive impact only in high-income countries. Yet, Assertiveness showed an opposite impact (negative) in low-income countries.

This study has crucial implications that should interest policy makers, entrepreneurs, and researchers. It offers policy makers a more macro understanding of the root causes in an aim to tackle them. Practitioners should also benefit from such a strategic overview that concerns the location of their existing/intended ventures. Researchers could also build upon and benefit from a more integrative study on the "why" and "how" of this relationship; described as a gap in literature. It challenges some widely-accepted concepts as well as solves a number of contradictory findings.

ACKNOWLEDGMENTS

With sincere gratitude and appreciation, I am humbly obliged to thank those who have helped me during the long, yet unmistakably inspiring, journey with this Doctorate dissertation. First of all, I would like to thank my supervisor Dr. Cristina Cruz for her valuable time, patience, dedication, and for generously sharing her vast knowledge and contagious passion for entrepreneurship and family business. I will always appreciate her mentorship and cherish her friendship. I am also grateful to Dr. Julio de Castro for his continuous support and constructive advice. And to Dr. Angel Diaz for his indispensable guidance and critical assistance throughout my time at the school. And to Dr. Joseph Pistrui for further provoking my curiosity in this field. And to Dr. Oswaldo Lorenzo for showing me how to prevent academic research from losing touch with reality. A special thanks should also be made to Dr. Elena Revilla for relentlessly motivating me and helping me stay in the right direction. I am also indebted to the advice and support given to me by Dr. Luis Gomez-Mejia and Dr. Alberto Maydeu.

I will always be indebted to the instrumental support and care given to me and all my colleagues from the brilliant team at the Doctorate Department; lead by the very kind Ms Laura Maguire and supported by Ms Ancir Salazar and Ms Iraida Jimenez. I would like to also thank my school at-large, professors, colleagues, and staff for giving me this terrific opportunity to learn – and surely give back - in such a perfect environment. I am also obliged to thank Dean Dr. Santiago Iniguez for consistently leading the school to and keeping it at the very competitive top. I also thank him for his continuous advice, support, and open-doors policy.

Last, but definitely not least, I would like to express my heartfelt appreciation to my ideal father; Sheikh/ Ahmed Al-Kadi for emotionally and financially supporting this and all of my endeavors in life. I would not be here without his unconditional generosity and leadership-by-example. I am also in great debt to my loving mother Madhawi Al-Kadi for her endless love, prayers, care and devotion. I would also never miss an opportunity to show the greatest appreciation to the love of my life; my wife Bedour. Thank you for your consistent love, sacrifices, self-denial, and patience during the ups and downs of the last years. Thank you for believing in me more than I do in myself! A special thanks is also due to all of my family, especially my brothers and sister; Yousef, Fawzi, Fahad, and Norah, for their constant help and love. My two sons, Saad and Meshari, this is for you – only if your mother approves!

1. INTRODUCTION

Since the early decades of last century, Schumpeter has been recognized to be among the first to highlight the importance and merit of studying entrepreneurship (Carland, Hoy, Boulton, & Carland, 1984) as the leading driver of economic growth and regional development (Chiles, Bluedorn, & Gupta, 2007). He argued that entrepreneurship is associated with the creation and destruction of industries as well as a major factor for economic development (Schumpeter, 1934). Entrepreneurship, according to him, is the "engine" of an economy and the process by which the economy as a whole goes forward (Stevenson & Jarillo, 1990; El-Harbi & Anderson, 2010). Today's world of increasing economic turbulence and challenges calls for entrepreneurs and entrepreneurial ventures that can successfully compete with national and international rivals (Ireland, Hitt, & Sirmon, 2003, Kuratko, 2007). In this vein, entrepreneurship has been subscribed by many scholars as a remedy that can hurl developing economies into economic dynamism (Berger, 1991). For example, the rapid industrialization of nations like the United States and Great Britain has been attributed to the development of the nations' entrepreneurial skills, which act as revitalizing and facilitating factors (Casson, 1990; Storey, 1994; Acs, 1992; Aronson, 1991; Oviatt & McDougall, 1994; Busenitz, Gomez, & Spencer, 2000).

Yet, despite the enormous literature and support for the instrumentality of entrepreneurship in stimulating economic growth, entrepreneurship flourishes in some countries whereas in others it does not (Acs, 2006, Audretsch & Thurik, 2000). The field scholars have observed that the level of entrepreneurial activity varies across both nations and over time (Verheul, Wennekers, Audretsch & Thurik, 2002; Rees & Shah, 1986; Blanchflower, 2000). And they have a limited understanding of *why* rates of entrepreneurship differ from one country to another (Aronson, 1991; Rondinelli & Kasarda, 1992). In response to this, Busenitz et al. (2000) argue that a greater understanding of *national differences* will help entrepreneurship researchers as well as would-be entrepreneurs, potential investors, and government policy makers, in trying to revitalize their national economies. Such *national differences* may constitute a very long list of differentiating factors, given the wide variety of nations and environments, e.g. economic and political policies, behavior of financial institutions, history, geographical location, etc. However, it appears that certain *cultural values* have consistently been associated with increased entrepreneurship levels, despite other *similarities* in economic and social realities among nations (e.g. McGrath, MacMillan, & Scheinberg, 1992).

Shapero & Sokol (1982) observed that business formation rates vary from a society to another. They argue that this is due to the fact that different cultures carry different beliefs about the desirability and feasibility of initiating new enterprises. These beliefs help determine which actions will be seriously considered and implemented (McGrath, MacMillan, & Scheinberg, 1992). There is a wealth of studies that emphasize the role and influence of cultural values and beliefs on the entrepreneurship environment and development (e.g. Davidsson, 1995; Davidsson & Wiklund, 1997; Begley & Tan, 2001; Busenitz & Lau, 1997; Knight, 1997; Tiessen, 1997); indicating that "culture does make a difference" (McGrath, MacMillan, & Scheinberg, 1992:117). However, despite the strong arguments in the field that ratify the culture as an important determinant of the level of entrepreneurship across nations and societies, there are relatively few *empirical* studies that focus on this issue (Davidsson, 1995; Davidsson & Wiklund, 1997; Hayton, George & Zahra, 2002). And even on the *theoretical* side, Mitchell, Smith, Seawright, & Morse (2000) argue that researchers have not reached an agreement on explanations of entrepreneurial activity within cultures (Shane, 1996), let alone across cultures (McDougall & Oviatt, 1997). George & Zahra (2002:5) observe that there are "...substantial components and manifestations of culture and its contingent influence on entrepreneurial outcomes [that] are yet unexplored, providing new opportunities for scholarly inquiry".

In tackling this issue, a number of researchers have studied: the cultural values and beliefs that differentiate entrepreneurs from non-entrepreneurs across nations (Fagenson, 1993; McGrath, MacMillan, & Scheinberg, 1992; McGrath & MacMillan, 1992) and within a nation (Davidsson, 1995; Davidsson & Wiklund, 1997), a single cultural phenomenon that differentiates the interest of two cultures in entrepreneurship (Begley & Tan, 2001), the stability or changing behavior of entrepreneurship-related cultural aspects (McGrath, MacMillan, Yang, & Tsai, 1992), the impact of culture on the strategic choices of entrepreneurial firms (Steensma, Marino, Weaver, & Dickson, 2000), and an analysis of the individual-level value system of entrepreneurs across cultures (Busenitz & Lau, 1997). Nonetheless, very little is known about the cultures that produce the high/low supply of entrepreneurs and entrepreneurial ventures in a given nation relative to other nations. In other words, we know that entrepreneurs are different from non-entrepreneurs, no matter of their respective cultures (e.g. McGrath & MacMillan, 1992), but their differences may well be due to their existing role and context. Their traits, value system, and cultural profile may have been a result of their existing reality as entrepreneurs; their status quo. This does not tell us about the macro, country-level cultural dimensions and environment that accepted, encouraged, and produced such high/low supply of entrepreneurs - instead the result of it. Entrepreneurs will be found in almost every nation, but nations may differ, however, in the culture that could affect the relative portion of the entrepreneurs (supply), and the cultural dimensions that help or hinder entrepreneurial activity. The cultural dimensions, in the literature, represent the manifestations/illustration of the values and practices of a certain culture. They illustrate the level of compliance/agreement or deviation/disagreement of a certain culture towards such dimension relative to other cultures. And in addition to the fact that studies on this topic are scarce, the findings are still extremely contradictory – as it could be observed in the Literature Review of this dissertation.

Building on the entrepreneurship and culture literature, this dissertation aims to develop a theoretical justification and an empirical assessment of the national culture's influence on the systematic variation of national aggregate entrepreneurial activity across nations. It aims to uncover the cultural dimensions that influence the level of entrepreneurship (in the nation level of analysis); identifying the ones that are associated with higher entrepreneurial activity (functional/fostering) and the ones that are associated with lower activity (dysfunctional/inhabiting). The study also aims to evaluate the available measurements of the entrepreneurship and national culture constructs; suggesting the most appropriate ones and criticizing some of the handicapped, yet popular, measurements. This is aimed to respond to the established theoretical argument that cultural variation is a determinant of cross-national variation in the "supply" of entrepreneurship (Davidsson & Wiklund, 1997) and the scholars' call to explore whether culture makes a difference at the country level of analysis (McGrath, MacMillan, Yang, & Tsai, 1992).

This dissertation paper has a number of implications that should interest academic researchers, national policy makers, and professional practitioners. It will add to the fields of entrepreneurship and sociology by assessing the national cultural dimensions/factors that foster or inhibit the aggregate entrepreneurship levels; shedding light on the still dark and vague side that ignited/obstructed such activity in the first place. It aspires to justify and solve a number of contradicting findings as well as establish new relationships with cultural dimensions that have never been directly associated with entrepreneurship. National policy makers should also benefit from this study as they will recognize the cultural dimensions that are affecting the revitalization of their economies from an entrepreneurial development perspective. Governments and policy makers around the world have acknowledged the fruitful consequences of encouraging entrepreneurship and have tried to develop the training and education programs that incentivize it. Nevertheless, the real positive impact of such endeavors has been questioned (Mueller, Thomas, & Jaeger, 2002), since most overlook their fitness to local contexts (Dubini, 1988; Davidsson, Lindmark, & Olofsson, 1994). Therefore, a better understanding of the underlying cultural dynamics and contextual realities of the nations' respective cultures will aid policy makers in developing the proper educational systems, economic policies, and cultural awareness campaigns that are relevant and tackle the roots of such phenomena. This will also result in a more efficient allocation of national resources and efforts – towards the areas that matter the most. Professional practitioners; entrepreneurs and potential entrepreneurs, will also be able to gain a better comprehension of particular factors or threats that are critical to the existence of their ventures. It will allow them to recognize essential dynamics that come into action and are crucial to the introduction and sustainability of their entrepreneurial ventures; for example, in aspects of finding the needed entrepreneurial human resources, cultural acceptability of such start-ups, and the general attitudes of the collective community. It could also aid their assessment and set their expectations when aiming to evaluate a location for their new ventures.

2. LITERATURE REVIEW

2.1. Entrepreneurship:

The earliest know definition of the entrepreneur, as it is recognized today, is that brought by Cantillon (circa 1700) who described the entrepreneurial individual as "a rational decision maker who assumed the risk and provided management for the firm" (Kilby, 1971 – cited in Carland et al., 1984). Since then, researchers have produced a long list of definitions for the concepts of entrepreneurship and the entrepreneur that meet each researcher's direction and intention in using these terms. For example, Gartner (1985) and Brockhaus (1987) define entrepreneurs in the lines of "individuals who initiated an entrepreneurial event, starting a venture" (McGrath, MacMillan, & Scheinberg, 1992). Entrepreneurship, on the other hand, has been defined by Vesper (1983:1) as "the creation of new independent businesses". In the same vein, two reviews of the literature (Low & MacMillan, 1988; Wortman, 1987) came to define entrepreneurship as the "creation of new organizations"; a definition I shall adopt in this dissertation due to its representation of the field's general trend and agreement (Thomas & Mueller, 2000; Begley & Tan, 2001).

Entrepreneurs have been characterized by a number of traits and qualities that differentiate them from small business managers. McClelland (1961) emphasized the entrepreneur's differentiating qualities of high need for achievement – namely preferences for challenge, acceptance of personal responsibility for outcomes, and innovativeness – and need for autonomy and independence. In the same vein, Begley & Boyd (1987) argued that entrepreneurs/founders scored significantly higher than small business managers/non-founders in need for achievement, risk-taking propensity, and tolerance of ambiguity. In reviewing a number of studies in this matter, Brockhaus (1982) and Gupta & Fernandez (2009) detected three consistently-reported attributes associated with entrepreneurial behavior, which are the need for achievement, internal locus of control, and risk-taking propensity. We can observe from this that the entrepreneurial value system and profile have consistently been associated with risk taking, need for achievement, need for independence, and uncertainty acceptance. However, this does not tell us, yet, about the culture and environment that produces such entrepreneurial individuals in larger numbers compared to other cultures. In short, we don't know what culture composition is the ideal one for stimulating the cross-over of its members to the "entrepreneurial land".

2.2. National Culture:

While the culture concept has been borrowed from anthropology to help understand and analyze many economical phenomena, there is still no consensus on its definition and boundaries (e.g. McGrath, MacMillan, Yang, & Tsai, 1992). Therefore, it should be no surprise to see that there is a variety of concepts and applications of culture in the literature (Smircich, 1983). Its meaning and implications are characterized by the context it is studied under – whether it is comparative management (cross-cultural), corporate culture, organizational cognition, organizational symbolism, unconscious processes, etc. Nevertheless, the focus of this study is geared towards the elements and definitions of culture that have an impact on entrepreneurship from a national perspective.

Since the anthropologist Redfield (1948) defined culture as a "shared understanding made manifest in act and artifact" (cited in House, Hanges, Javidan, Dorfman, & Gupta, 2004:xv), the definitions of culture followed the same idea but were tweaked towards the in-focus subject. Culture, according to anthropology researchers such as Kroeber & Parsons (1958) and Hall (1973), is related to the ways in which societies organize social behavior and knowledge (McGrath, MacMillan, Yang, & Tsai, 1992). In his various papers, Hofstede's definition of culture seems to be popular among social and economics researchers. His analysis of culture and identification of its dimensions proved to be valuable to the study of entrepreneurial behavior and have been widely used by scholars in the field. According to Hofstede, culture is the "the collective programming of the mind that distinguishes the members of one group or category of people from another" (Hofstede, 2001:9), while a review paper define it briefly as a "set of shared values, beliefs, and expected behaviors" (Hayton et al., 2002:33). A more recent definition is the one proposed by the GLOBE Study's researchers, which builds on Hofstede's conceptualization and was agreed upon by a large number of researchers in the field; they define it as the "shared motives, values, beliefs, identities, and interpretations or meanings of significant events that result from common experiences of members of collectives that are transmitted across generations" (House et al., 2004:15). This definition stresses on the culture's semi-sustainable nature, distinguishing feature, and harmony of source and interpretation.

The definitions of culture imply that it can be used for indentifying and distinguishing any semi-homogeneous group that shares common beliefs and interpretations. Hence, the concept of culture could be employed at varying levels; e.g. organizational culture, family culture, specific ethnic culture, immigrant culture, etc. However, a number of researchers consent that *nations (or countries)* provide us with probably the only kinds of viable units available for comparing cultures (Hofstede, 2001). Kluckhohn & Strodtbeck (1961) argue that "national culture is a fairly consistent set of value orientations developed in response to the fact that there are a limited number of common societal problems with a limited number of known responses" (McGrath, MacMillan, Yang, & Tsai, 1992:443). In their recent review of the field, Engelen, Heinemann, & Brettel (2009) emphasized the role of *national* culture as an important *boundary* parameter for the study of entrepreneurship. Nations are capable of creating tenuous ties that form shared perceptions even though members of this group might not know one another (e.g. attitudes towards business or a sports team that are very specific to a region). Hofstede (2001) also argue that national borders are the most suitable for cultural comparisons because mechanisms promoting cultural similarities such as the educational and law systems, as well as the language, are usually shared at the national level. Therefore, at the national level, entrepreneurs as well as entrepreneurial organizations share a large portion of similarities (Engelen et al., 2009; Geroge & Zahra, 2002). These shared perceptions will lead to relatively similar behaviors and outcomes, shaped by the society's regional culture and historical experiences (Davis, Pitts, & Cormier, 2000; Ward, 2000). Despite other available levels of analysis and boundaries for culture, nations provide us with the best available and attainable boundary that allow us to explain different entrepreneurial activity levels (Weber, 1904).

It is important to note that a nation's culture may constitutes a number of sub-cultures that distinguish common groups (e.g. regions, religions, ethnicities), yet it allows us to grasp the aggregate and average cultural profile of that nation. This, in turn, allows us to assess the prevailing culture (with consideration to its components' varying degrees of conformity) in that nation. Any judgment or conclusion that stems from such conceptualization of culture should not be, however, assumed to be true for other levels of analysis such as the individual level or sub-group level. Failing to acknowledge the distinction between the individual (or sub-group) and the nation levels of analysis constitutes what was termed "ecological fallacy" (Hofstede, 1980; 2001). Hofstede suggested that culture is to collectivity what personality is to an individual; which means that it is "the interactive aggregate of common characteristics that influence a human group's response to its environment" (2001:10).

2.3. Review of the Construct Measurements:

There is a crucial issue when pursuing any cross-country study; that is the comparability of data, which is true for any measure. Databases in different countries/cultures do not often use uniformed classifications and data (Engelen et al., 2009). For example, using reported rates (e.g. self-employment rates, firm formation) from different countries may constitutes biases depending on the methodology used by each country (or agency) in collecting such data. Hofstede (2001) argue that using well-matched samples in cross-cultural research is important when researchers are interested in similarities and differences between national cultures. The standardized uniformity and symmetry of data collection and methodology are essential to achieve reliability and make a more informative sense of the data. Such methodological challenges should be well acknowledged when undergoing a wide cross-national study.

2.3.1. Measuring Entrepreneurship:

In an effort to operationalize the construct of entrepreneurship across countries, researchers have employed a number of measures that vary in their validity and reliability to capture this concept. Some popular measures are: the publicly-reported firm formation rates (e.g. Davidsson, 1995) and the self-employment rate (e.g. El-Harbi & Anderson, 2010) among other measures. However, these measures seem to have their limitations; some which are severe. For example, the *publicly-reported firm formation rates* do not include non-registered firms. They most probably also include firms that are "on paper" only, some which may serve as vehicles for acquisitions or equity holding, some which are partners' trusts, and others which may be new registrations for existing companies (when changing the configuration of shareholders, for instance, or changing the legal structure). In reality, not all of these "newly-formed" entities are made with an entrepreneurial aim. As such, this indicatory rates fall short in properly measuring entrepreneurial venture creation levels.

The other example is *self-employment rate*, which may also be misleading. Self-employment data is normally collected through self-reporting or government-reporting of individuals who indicate that they are self-employed. There is a number of issues with these figures. Firstly, there would normally be a number of individuals who work together as partners and all report themselves as self-employed, resulting in multiple data entries. This is an issue that may overestimate the level of venture creation in one country where such partnerships are more common than other countries. Secondly, a self-employed individual does not necessarily mean he/she is an entrepreneur or a founder. This self-employed individual may have inherited or bought an existing business, not necessarily initiating a new venture. Thirdly, many jobless individuals may label themselves as self-employed, although not actually running and committing themselves to a venture. It may also be a status of the *"between jobs"* individuals. Fourthly, self-employment may mean that some individuals work as one-person consultants, freelancers, or expert retirees. This is a one-man show that does not resemble an organized enterprise. It is merely a legal entity at best. Fifthly, this categorization overlooks the founding of newly-established large ventures, where the shareholders may be other companies or the public – or corporate entrepreneurship.

The above efforts to measure the entrepreneurship construct may well be the best available options if we have not attained a good alternative. The GEM program (Global Entrepreneurship Monitor) was developed to address the need for information about entrepreneurial activity around the world (www.gemconsortium. org). Since 1999, the GEM program has reported differences in levels of entrepreneurial activity among countries (Reynolds, Camp, Bygrave, Autio, & Hay, 2001). In offering comparable rates of entrepreneurship across countries, this program has made the possibility of analyzing entrepreneurship-related topics a much more achievable endeavor (Baughn, Chua, & Neupert, 2006). With the support of a number of leading business schools, the project aims to make sure that the empirical assessment of national entrepreneurial activity and data collection process are uniformed across countries. In pursuing this ambitious goal, the project has engaged academic national teams from more than 50 countries to collect data in a unified manner that harmonizes the comparison of entrepreneurship across countries. Every team has undergone a representative population-wide survey as well as an input from a panel of national experts to reflect the country level status of entrepreneurship. The project provides a number of interesting findings and annually-updated measures. However, the most relevant measure to this dissertation paper is the TEA (Early-Stage Total Entrepreneurial Activity), which gauges the actual levels of creating new entrepreneurial ventures in a percentage-of-population form. It is defined as the "the proportion of people aged 18-64 who are involved in entrepreneurial activity as a nascent entrepreneur or as an owner-manager of a new business" (e.g. GEM Executive Report 2009). It is important to note that such project measures entrepreneurship directly through the responses of sampled adult individuals, not through secondary data or governmental records. Although the project initially has faced a shy acceptance from researchers in the field, it is currently gaining more credibility. At present, GEM findings have been used in more than 80 peer-reviewed published papers, 12 dissertations, and 25 other academic papers (GEM-supplied list). For more information about GEM's data and methodology, see Reynolds, Bosma, Autio, De Bono, Servais, Lopez-Garcia, & Chin (2005).

2.3.2. *Measuring National Culture:*

The majority of behavioral studies – including entrepreneurship – have employed interpretations of Hofstede's famous cultural dimensions when studying culture (Hayton et al., 2002; Businetz et al., 2000; Engelen et al., 2009; George & Zahra, 2002; Licht & Siegel, 2005). Geert Hofstede's early conceptualization of culture and its dimensions (Hofstede, 1980, 1983a, 1983b, 1983c, 1983d, 2001) was modeled after a project that covered differences among national cultures through a study carried out on the employees of IBM and its subsidiaries in more than fifty countries (for a review of the study, see: Hofstede, Neuijen, Ohayv, & Sanders, 1990). He originally developed four cultural dimensions (*individualism/collectivism, uncertainty avoidance, power distance, and masculinity/femininity*), then added an independent fifth dimension derived from the Eastern cultures. This dimension, *"Confucian dynamism"*, opposes a *long-term to short-term orientation* in life and work, which gained popularity provided the remarkable success in the 1970s and 1980s of the East-Asian countries (Hofstede & Bond, 1988; Bond & Pang, 1989). These five dimensions were expected to provide "collective mental programs" that legitimize acceptable values and behaviors (Sharma & Manikutty, 2005). Although his early studies were focused on the organizational culture, the findings and further refinements proved to be, at least, conservative estimates of differences among the national populations at large - as respondents are supposed to share the same worldwide corporate culture (Hofstede et al., 1990). In describing national cultures, these aggregate indicators try to aid researchers in comparing the average scores of each nation, instead of each individual.

Despite the popularity of Hofstede's conceptualization of culture, there seem to be a number of crucial criticisms to the adoption of his data; which made some describe it as possibly inaccurate (e.g. Shane, 1993). For instance, a study has found that ambient temperature, rather than national culture (measured through Hofstede's dimensions), better explain role stresses (van de Vilert & van Yperen, 1996). Busenitz et al. (2000) found that papers using Hofstede's measure of culture, alone, do not adequately describe cross-country differences in entrepreneurial activity. The almost exclusive reliance on and undifferentiated use of this dataset has been seen to require serious criticism (Engelen et al., 2009). George & Zahra (2002) also argue that although Hofstede's dimensions served the field well, there is a need to discover other measures that capture the rich variety of national cultures. So, some have questioned its relevance to the study of entrepreneurship (Engelen et al., 2009). In the following, I summarize the main issues with regards to the application of Hofstede's dimensions to entrepreneurship assessment (and other areas of scientific investigation) across countries:

a. Despite the relatively recent aims to generalize the study from the same set of data to the country level of analysis, Hofstede's project was initially intended to study the organizational culture of IBM across its subsidiaries for the sake of HR analysis and internal corporate policy making.

b. The sample was exclusively composed of corporate executives and employees of a single mature corporation (IBM), instead of a random sample from the wide population. This assumes that the interaction of cultural values and tendency to work at IBM is constant across all countries, which is not proven (Shane,1993). Hence, this naturally limits the generalization and representation of this sample and data to the individuals who chose to work for IBM.

c. The classification of dimensions and the actual gathered data of countries are developed more than 40 years ago, which questions their validity today. Without an examination of the change in his cultural ratings overtime, we cannot assume they are valid today (Shane, 1992). According to Hofstede (2001), the uncertainty avoidance dimension levels, for instance, do fluctuate over time.

d. The measurements do not differentiate between the culture's values and actual practices of its members. According to House et al. (2004), Hofstede has either included items that focus only on practices (Hofstede et al., 1990) or a mix of both in the same scale (Hofstede, 1980); which confuses – or at least limits – the understanding of the studied phenomenon.

e. There seems to be some mixed dimensions that confuses researchers (McGrath, MacMillan, & Scheinberg, 1992); such as the masculinity dimension. Although the name and some of its components imply that it accounts for the gender equality or roles, it also incorporates some debatably unrelated concepts; such as the "value of hard work". Such "value of hard work" is not exclusively a masculine attribute as suggested. Individuals can be of either gender and still have a high or low value of hard work. It seems that this dimension, misleadingly, measures more than one independent differentiating dimension.

f. Missing information on countries from important and distinctive cultures (e.g. Middle East/Arab) that may prove to be useful for comparison and analysis. Hofstede justified this by his limitation to countries where IBM was actively working in and his unfortunate loss of some important datasets (Hofstede, 2001).

In an attempt to offer an alternative tool to tackle this issue, Busenitz et al. (2000) proposed a three-dimensional measure of "country institutional profiles" that contain the regulatory, cognitive, and normative aspects that are expected to influence levels of entrepreneurship across cultures. Even though this approach does explicitly recognize that country differences, contain more than the normative aspect of culture, and it focuses solely on factors influencing entrepreneurship, it fails to find consistency across countries – which meant that this model is probably country or culture specific (Hayton et al., 2002).

Building on Hofstede and other researchers' work, a new global project has taken place to identify the main cultural values and practices that distinguish nations and societies from each other. The 10-year GLOBE Study (Global Leadership and Organizational Behavior Effectiveness Research Program) of 62 nations has collected responses from about 17,300 individuals throughout the world, and was complemented by interviews, focus group discussions, and formal content analysis of printed media. In the GLOBE Study's published book (House et al., 2004; House, Javidan, & Dorfman, 2001), the authors describe and analyze how each of the 62 societies (with at least three countries from each major geographical region of the world) scores on nine major attributes of culture, namely: *Performance Orientation, Uncertainty Avoidance, Humane Orientation, Institutional Collectivism, In-Group Collectivism, Assertiveness, Gender Egalitarianism, Future Orientation, and Power Distance*. When quantified, these attributes are referred to as cultural dimensions. Although there is a number of overlapping dimensions with Hofstede's work, there are some important ones that are not directly covered by him (e.g. Assertiveness, Performance Orientation, Gender Egalitarianism, Humane Orientation, In-Group and Institutional Collectivism). And in contrast to most studies of culture that focus and report on the values of societies only, the GLOBE study adds to this tradition by examining both *values* (the "should be") and actual *practices* (the "as is"). In addition to the respective countries' cultural profiling, they also group countries with similar cultural scores into 10 culturally-relative, validated clusters (namely; Anglo, Germanic Europe, Confucian Asia, Sub-Saharan Africa, Middle East, Southern Asia, Eastern Europe, Latin Europe, Nordic Europe, and Latin America). The GLOBE Study's findings confirmed that while significant inter-firm differences in organizational cultures exist, the societal differences account for more than 50% of these differences. The clusters, on the other hand, account for more than 50% of the inter-societal differences in cultures (Gupta, Levenburg, Moore, Motwani, & Schwarz, 2008).

This ambitious and validated research project offers systematic, comparable, and comprehensive data on the issue of national culture as the field has rarely seen before. It allows researchers to relate different phenomena with the cultural patterns present across nations, which permits this study to test its propositions with regard to the associations of national culture to entrepreneurship, in an aggregate, country-level approach. It also offers us a number of new cultural dimensions that could be associated with entrepreneurship, yet never been tested, e.g. Assertiveness, Performance Orientation, and In-Group/ Institutional Collectiveness. In an aim to overcome the above-discussed shortfalls of Hofstede's measures, this project offers researchers the following advantages:

- The project's plan, scope, and execution were all intended to study national culture, instead of the IBM organizational culture – where the level of analysis is the country.

- The sample selection was not limited to one company.

- The collected data is relatively recent (or at least more recent) and; hence, should be more relevant and accurate.

- It clearly differentiates and independently measures the two distinct facets of culture; values (the "should be") and practices ("as is").

- It provides more precise conceptualizations of the cultural dimensions, overcoming many of the overlapping and mixing problems present in some commonly-used dimensions.

- It is not limited by the countries where one company operates in. This has allowed it to cover varying cultures (62 nations representing 10 cultural clusters from 6 continents).

Engelen et al. (2009) advance that researches could benefit from such study in order to substantiate or modify Hofstede's older classifications and in questioning whether the additional dimensions are better suited for the concerned research topic. They further advance that "as Hofstede's dimensions were empirically derived in the context of a large and mature organization, entrepreneurship research could highly benefit from the broader choice" (2009:178). Hence, this dissertation aims to exploit the valuable information and findings of this global research project in the test of hypotheses.

A review of the definitions of culture and its dimensions by Hofstede and GLOBE is presented in (Appendix A) at the end of this paper.

2.4. Review of Empirical Studies:

In spite of the crucial impact of national culture on the economies of nations and their entrepreneurship levels, researchers have agreed that systematic studies in this regard are scarce and/or difficult to carry out (Berger, 1991; Davidsson, 1995; Begley & Tan, 2001; Davidsson & Wiklund, 1997; Davidsson & Wiklund, 2001). Hayton et al. (2002), in their review of the entrepreneurship/culture nexus, observed that the literature seems to follow three research streams; namely:

1) The impact of national culture on the aggregate measures of entrepreneurship.

2) The association between national culture and the characteristics of individual entrepreneurs.

3) The impact of national culture on corporate entrepreneurship.

This dissertation paper can be classified in the first stream of literature, where – according to the previous review - only few empirical studies have examined the association between dimensions of culture and entrepreneurship at the national level (Davidsson, 1995; Davidsson & Wiklund, 1997; Shane, 1992, 1993). Hence, this following review shall focus on papers that tackle the relationship between culture and entrepreneurship at the national aggregate level only.

Two papers by Shane (1992; 1993) have investigated the influence of culture on the levels of innovation across a number of countries. His papers have examined the cultural dimensions that inhibit or encourage reported levels of innovation in both commercial and scientific applications. Although his papers (1992; 1993) were often reviewed under the stream of the "impact of national culture on aggregate measures of entrepreneurship" (e.g. Hayton et al., 2002), they are not directly associated with entrepreneurship. This is indeed surprising as Shane never made a direct association with it; instead with innovativeness of societies. Although innovation has been linked to entrepreneurship as one item among the traits of entrepreneurs (Mueller & Thomas, 2000), using per capita *patent filings* (or in the other study; per capita *number of trade marks*) as a proxy for the level of entrepreneurship in countries greatly questions the validity of such far-reaching assumption (Licht & Siegel, 2005). Using Hofstede's cultural dimensions, Shane (1992; 1993) found that high levels of individualism and low power distance in countries correlate with high innovativeness. His propositions, however, were supported for the time period of 1975, but not for 1980 – indicating that the association with Hofstede's cultural values may not be stable over time. He criticized Hofstede's measures by stating that they may be inaccurate (Shane, 1993); a point which was addressed in this paper's review of measurements. Shane's research, though, supports the notion that nations may differ (here; in innovation rates) because of the cultural values embraced by their citizens. This finding further endorses the possibility of finding a difference - in the case of entrepreneurship – as a result of the dissimilar national cultural profiles across countries.

In the same research stream, two other papers tackle the issue of culture and entrepreneurship (Davidsson, 1995; Davidsson & Wiklund, 1997). Both papers analyze the culture's influence on entrepreneurship within a single country; i.e. Sweden. The authors justified the decision to study one country only by the costly and difficult to attain cross-country data, language challenges, and structural conditions (Davidsson & Wiklund, 1997). They have selected three matched pairs of sub-regions of Sweden in order to control for structural factors. However, as an unfortunate consequence for their aim to control for this, they have created sub-regions with little cultural variation. Consequently, this has showed only marginal support for the influence of culture on new firm-formation rates in both papers. Moreover, Davidsson's (1995) selection of sub-regions was not based on cultural variation; instead, it was based on density and location. Therefore, we can argue that the reflection of the Swedish-only societal culture and this little variation do not serve best our aim to explain the cross-country cultural variations and consequences on entrepreneurship levels. There were also a number of crucial limitations in these papers. The sample coverage is small as it only covers individuals of the age groups 35-36 and 18-19 in Davidsson (1995) and 35-40 in Davidsson & Wiklund (1997). They presumed that this latter age group is the most relevant to new firm formation rates, which is a highly questionable claim. Their selection of specific "beliefs" items in the questionnaires was based on what they have called "common sense reasoning rather than established theories of previous research findings" (1997:186) – some were very Swedish-centric like the "Jante-mentality" measure (Davidsson & Wiklund, 1997). Another issue is that their culture data was collected in 1994 and the firm formation rates data was for the years 1985-89; where they assumed full stability of culture. Due to the little support for their propositions, they have argued that it "may be debated if this research is to be called exploratory" (Davidsson

& Wiklund, 1997:186). The authors also conclude by saying that "with regard to particular values or beliefs, we are unable to point out specific aspects of regional culture which consistently appear as a determinant of the new firm formation rate" (1997:193). In their own justification for this weak support, they questioned the validity of their culture measure, their entrepreneurship measure (firm formation rate), the use of questionnaires in data collection, and the selection of regions. They also indicate that the main reason for this weak relationship is that the country seems to be culturally homogeneous; where a constant cannot explain variations. Moreover, both papers do not contain any proposed hypotheses or testing. Therefore, I presume that this study cannot really assist us in fully understanding the different cultures' impact on entrepreneurship. This study, however, may serve as an exploratory research for the sub-regions of Sweden. Given the limited cultural variation in Sweden and the little support for their propositions, the authors recommend that such relationship should be studied across countries (Davidsson & Wiklund, 1997) – which this dissertation aims to do.

Another study (Begley & Tan, 2001) was aimed to predict interest in entrepreneurship using a single cultural variable that distinguishes between East Asian and Anglo-Saxon cultures. Using the "theory of face[1]", the authors found that the "social status of entrepreneurship" and "shame from business failure"

---

[1] Earley (1997) defines face as "the evaluation of self based on internal and external judgments concerning a person's adherence to moral rules of conduct and position within a given social structure" (p. 43). He proposed that face is central to people's self-definitions relative to the larger social structures in which they are embedded in. His theory of face stems from the Chinese heritage, in which two kinds of face are identified, *lian* (moral character) and *mianzi* (external prestige) (Begley & Tan, 2001).

do predict interest in entrepreneurship better in East Asian than Anglo-Saxon countries. Their sample consisted of MBA students at a number of countries from the two cultures. The findings are interesting and shed light on a new construct that have not been historically found in western societies. However, the study gives us an insightful scope on only one cultural phenomenon that makes an impact on one wide culture (six countries labeled under the East Asian culture). Moreover, the impact of such variable has been recorded according to the sampled students' *desire to engage in an entrepreneurial endeavor*. This also does not tell us about the actual activity and action towards firm formation or entrepreneurship. So, the partial cultural justification (one variable impacting one multiple-countries' culture) and the non-actual entrepreneurial activity (willingness, interest) limits the contribution of this paper to our goal in this dissertation.

A more recent article by Wu (2007) was aimed to find a relationship between national culture and national entrepreneurial activity across countries. Using four of Hofstede's cultural dimensions, the study failed to find a relationship except for the individualism dimension. Surprisingly, individualism was found to be negatively related to entrepreneurial activity. This, indeed, is a contradictive finding to the author's expectations as well as most of the literature on this topic, where entrepreneurship is believed to flourish in individualistic cultures. However, all of the paper's hypotheses concerning the other dimensions were not supported. Moreover, it seems that there is more than 20-years time gap between the date of the culture data and entrepreneurship data. This may be one of the reasons for not finding a relationship. Additionally, the author's utilization of Hofstede's cultural dimensions may constitutes another reason.

Although Hofstede's conceptualization of culture has been fairly widespread among researchers in a number of fields, his actual data seems not to be the best available to give a close-to-reality picture of countries. The reasons for this argument have been discussed in the measurement review section.

Another paper that uses Hofstede's four dimensions is by Mueller et al. (2002), who studied the impact of culture on the entrepreneurial *potential* among university students. The authors constructed an individual entrepreneurial orientation (potential) measure, which constituted the items of innovativeness and locus of control. Contrary to the paper by Wu (2007), they found that none of Hofstede's cultural dimensions, except masculinity, were associated with a higher entrepreneurial potential among students in 17 countries. The paper found that countries with high masculinity cultures seemed to have more propensity for engaging in entrepreneurial activities. However, the paper was measuring for the students' potential to engage in entrepreneurial activities in the future, which does not capture the reality of entrepreneurial activity. Due to the use of such limited-in-generalization sample, the focus on the potentiality of pursuing an entrepreneurial activity, the limitations in covering a wide range of distinctive cultures, and the employment of Hofstede's data, there is a need for a more insightful and relevant study. The authors also recommended studying such cultural values with regard to the *actual* entrepreneurship levels across countries, which this dissertation aims to tackle.

A summary of this review of empirical studies can be seen in (Appendix B) at the end of this paper.

In their review, Hayton et al. (2002) concluded that high individualism, high masculinity, low uncertainty avoidance, and low power distance seem to be supportive to entrepreneurship. However, the evidence for such conclusion seems to be mixed (Licht & Siegel, 2005) and even contradictory as seen in the above reviewed papers and wide literature. I argue that these mixed or contradictory findings can be traced to a number of factors, namely:

- The lack of solid theoretical foundations for the proposed relationships.

- The improper use of some misleading proxy measures of entrepreneurship and/or culture.

- The improper generalization of one-country's findings and context to all countries.

- The tendency to focus on one aspect of culture only.

- The inadequate sample size and sample coverage of different cultures.

- The limited availability and usage of comparable data on culture and entrepreneurship from different countries.

- The reliance on American-endorsed and acclaimed entrepreneurial and cultural values that may not be relevant or applicable to all cultures.

2.5. Contributions:

Despite the significance and instrumentality of entrepreneurship as an "engine" of economic prosperity, and the culture's wide influence on the acceptance and formation of entrepreneurial ventures, few studies have been conducted to tackle this issue in the field (George & Zahra, 2002; Begley & Tan, 2001; Hayton et al., 2002; Davidsson, 1995; Busenitz et al., 2000). Many classical theorists such as Adam Smith, Karl Marx, and Max Weber have discussed the influential role played by culture in motivating economic activity (Begley & Tan, 2001). And in the particular case of entrepreneurship, many recent researchers have substantiated the role of culture in impacting the entrepreneurial environment and development (e.g. Shapero & Sokol, 1982). Nevertheless, Davidsson & Wiklund (1997) state that "systematic empirical research on this conception of culture on the one hand, and rates of new firm formation on the other, is scarce". Hence, researchers have agreed that the scarcity of studies on the culture's impact constitutes a *gap* in the entrepreneurship literature (e.g. Berger, 1991; Davidsson, 1995; Begley & Tan, 2001).

In an aim to fill this gap and attend to the shortcomings of the scarce and handicapped studies on this topic (as mentioned above), this dissertation aims to:

a. Establish a solid theoretical link between national culture and aggregate levels of entrepreneurship across countries that builds on the literature of the two research fields.

b. Introduce new relationships of cultural dimensions that have never been studied to have an influence on entrepreneurship; through theoretical justification and empirical testing.

c. Rationalize the contradictory findings of already-studied cultural dimensions through theoretical arguments and subsequent testing of these propositions.

d. Criticize popular measures of the constructs of national culture and entrepreneurship. And assessing the more fitting alternative measures with due justification.

e. Introduce a possibility to combine and make sense of the findings and data of two global research projects (GLOBE and GEM); in a relevant and valuable contributory study to the fields of sociology and entrepreneurship.

In doing so, this dissertation paper aims to introduce new relationships, solve the paradox of previous contradictory findings as well as suggest a more comprehensive assessment of the national culture's impact on the aggregate level of entrepreneurship. Theoretically, it will seek to establish a connection between the different national culture dimensions (some have never been directly associated with entrepreneurship) and national levels of entrepreneurial activity. And empirically, it will refine the handicapped and mixed results with regards to this connection as well as assess the most fitting construct measurements.

3. THEORETICAL BACKGROUND AND HYPOTHESES

3.1. Theoretical Background:

Since it could be observed that different cultures have different attitudes toward business formation (e.g. Shapero & Sokol, 1982), an understanding of the way cultures influence such attitudes needs to be addressed. It should first be agreed that entrepreneurs act within a society and their entrepreneurial process is shaped by that society (Anderson & Miller, 2003; Anderson & Smith, 2007; El-Harbi & Anderson, 2010). Mueller & Thomas (2000) argue that culture – as the underlying distinctive system of values to its members – leads to the development of certain personality traits and incentivizes individuals in a society to engage in behaviors that may not be evident in other societies. Entrepreneurship activity is one of these behaviors which vary across countries due to differences in cultural values and beliefs. Hence, we would expect that some cultures may promote entrepreneurial characteristics among its members, and other cultures may penalize it. The consequence of this may be apparent in the nation's overall entrepreneurship activity levels. In other words, while borrowing Hofstede's terminology, entrepreneurship is a "consequence" of a certain culture (Hofstede, 2001). Attempting to study managerial decisions and processes while ignoring societal culture has been portrayed as "a trivial pursuit" (Hofstede, 2001, p. 240). Two threads of research theories could grant us more insight into this relationship; namely, cognition and institutional theories.

3.1.1. Cognitive Justifications:

In describing how cultural values shape the entrepreneurial activity, Cochran (1949) supported the idea of culture as a *causal force* that influences the incidence and form of entrepreneurship. He argued that beliefs are basically manifestations of deeper logic filtered through the material realities faced in the immediate context (Elam & Terjesen, 2007). The stream of research on cognition and cognitive maps supports the theorized interaction between values and the development of new ventures (Louis, 1980; Busenitz & Lau, 1997). In their review, Adler, Doktor, & Redding (1986) noted that national culture, mediated through cognitive maps, is an important predictor of behavior, and that this connection is an important cornerstone in cross-cultural research. Busenitz & Lau (1997) have modeled a cognitive explanation of new venture creation; where the national culture impacts the individual mindset and sensemaking in the venture-creation decision through a restraining or promoting set of cultural values. The various cultural values present in any nation influence the perception of an individual or group through *cognitive schema* (Shaw, 1990), *interpretation* (Daft & Weick, 1984), and *sensemaking* (Weick, 1995 – cited in Baker, Gedajlovic, & Lubatkin, 2005). *Cognitive schema*, here, is defined as the "generalized cognitive structures or frameworks that people use to impose structure on an impart meaning to some particular event or domain" (Bartunek, 1984). Culture influences the content and structure of one's cognitive schema and the extent to which individuals process information in an automatic or controlled manner (Shaw, 1990), leading to a development of a "shared schema" or common patterns of thinking, responding, and interpreting stimuli they encounter (House et al., 2004). *Interpretation* is also another vital influencer of perception because every entrepreneurial activity or outcome is in some way dependent on interpretation, which is defined as the "stage wherein data are given meaning" (Daft & Weick, 1984). The last component is *sensemaking*, which Weick (1995) describes it as "the making of sense". The collective sensemaking builds shared perceptions at the group level (Morrison & Milliken, 2000; Young & Parker, 1999) and it is facilitated by identification with a certain group (Porac, Thomas, & Baden-Fuller, 1989). Thus, the perception of a worthy opportunity or the availability and feasibility of resources to capture it are all based on the entrepreneur's understanding of what is a "correct thing to do", given his/her current societal reality and context. This is also in line with the value-belief theory (Hofstede, 2001; Triandis, 1995), which states that "values and beliefs held by members of cultures influence the degree to which the behaviors of individuals, groups, and institutions within cultures are enacted, and the degree to which they are viewed as legitimate, acceptable, and effective" (House et al., 2004:17). Hence, cultural values play a vital role in giving meaning to many aspects of life (Hofstede, 1984) – where entrepreneurship is one of these life aspects.

3.1.2. *Institutional Justifications*

Culture, in essence, then "institutionalizes" the values that either accept/promote or reject/penalize certain behaviors and practices among its members. And since entrepreneurship is one of the culture's consequences, we can assume that the values and practices that go with it should be affected by such institutionalization. In this vein, the *institutional theory* refers to the role played by culture – through *social stimuli* - in shaping the undertaken actions (DiMaggio & Powell, 1983; Meyer & Rowan, 1977; Scott, 1995; Scott, 2005). According to the institutional theory, institutions (in this case, culture) shape the behavior of organizations - such as the entrepreneurial venture (North, 1991). In order to gain external legitimacy, it is assumed that organizations act within the acceptable/institutionalized norms, values, and routines of the environment they operate within (Granovetter, 1985) and reflect the values and norms of their societies (Zucker, 1977). Organizations also draw on the institution/culture's criteria in evaluating its organizational structures and not on their own, possibly efficiency-driven, criteria (Engelen et al., 2009; Scott & Meyer, 1991). In organizations, the decision to take action, interpret it, and share this interpretation with others replicate the society's broad order and behavior (Selznick, 1957; Shane, 1992). Firms that fail to live with such legitimizing rules and norms will be lead to die off (Shane, 1992). According to the institutional theory, culture's influence can be best seen in what were termed "coercive isomorphism" and "normative isomorphism". The first being the organizations' response to formal and informal pressures on them by the rest of organizations on which they are dependent as well as by the larger cultural expectations of the society in which they operate (DiMaggio & Powell, 1983; House et al., 2004). The latter pressure, "normative isomorphism", refers to the pressure to conformity exerted on organizations through common educational, training, and association contingencies of the organization's members. Such common influencers of behavior lay a foundation of similarity in decision making and responses to encountered problems. The education and professional associations, in turn, also reflect the wider culture's reality and context (DiMaggio & Powell, 1983; House et al., 2004).

Although the institutional theory primarily focuses on organizations rather than individuals (entrepreneurs), we can comfortably assume that entrepreneurs – as founders and leaders of newly-established firms – will act within this logic. Scott (1995; 2007) extends on the work by DiMaggio & Powell (1983), who may be considered among the most recognized researchers on this theory, by categorizing the three main institutional pillars: regulatory, normative, and cognitive. In their recent review of institutional theory and entrepreneurship, Bruton, Ahlstrom, & Li (2010) advance that "The normative pillar represents actions that organizations and individuals ought to take; normative pillars are the standards of behavior and commercial conventions of different professions, occupations, and organizational fields." A normative evaluation of legitimacy concerns whether the organization's activities are proper and consistent with influential groups and societal norms (Suchman, 1995). The cognitive institutional pillar includes the scripts, schemas, and taken-for-granted elements that influence individuals in a particular sociocultural context. A cognitive evaluation of legitimacy concerns the congruence between an organization and its cultural environment (Meyer & Scott, 1983). Culture is believed to be a mean where both *normative* and *cognitive* structures are transmitted (DiMaggio & Powell, 1991; Jepperson, 1991), where the individual mindset and behavior is impacted by such transmittance of institutionalized cultural values (Collins, 2004). This is also in line with the *societal legitimation* or *supportive environment* perspective argued by Etzioni (1987). Most importantly, the reviewers state that researchers who only focus on single countries may find it difficult to judge the impact of institutions. They argue that future research should assess and compare the impact of different institutional structures (different cultures) by including multiple countries in the research (Bruton et al., 2010). This dissertation aims to follow this recommendation by assessing the implications of different institutions (with different practices) in a wide range of countries.

The rationale used by the institutional theory can be matched perfectly with the theoretical conceptualization of culture in Hofstede's work (e.g. 2001). He argues that cultural patterns arise from the ways in which different groups deal with fundamental human problems. Cultural values, according to him, are the broad tendency to prefer certain states of affairs over others. These values have developed early in life, where they were "programmed" into people mindsets. Long-lasting values are, by nature, non-rational, and may even be contradictive, enduring, and acted upon in a semi-unconscious way. So, they are institutionalized in people's minds and behaviors (McGrath, MacMillan, & Scheinberg, 1992). The consequences of a particular culture (the institution) are seen in an institutionalized states of affairs or shared values that aid individuals in giving meaning to incidents around them. For example, a culture's shared value of high individualism, will make such society favor more press freedom and greater occupational mobility. Societies with low individualism (collectivist), on the other hand, may favor less press freedom, common identity and roots, and less occupational mobility (Hofstede, 2001; McGrath, MacMillan, & Scheinberg, 1992). Consequences of culture (such as entrepreneurship) are both created and reinforced by the underlying cultural conditions. The shared values represent the "legitimating" authority for any behavior or response to an incident. Potential entrepreneurs, like any individual, should conform to the apparent cultural values or they would be viewed with suspicion as "deviants" (Mueller & Thomas, 2000). Consequently, culture could be credited for influencing the supportiveness of the environment as to make it more legitimate to form a new business (Etzioni, 1987). Hence, the link between the national culture and the aggregate entrepreneurship levels in such culture seems to constitute a sound and rational assumption for further exploration.

3.2. Hypotheses:

Based on the above theorization of the cultural influence on the aggregate levels of entrepreneurial activity across nations, this dissertation proposes a number of hypotheses that can be tested within this theoretical justifications. I have argued that the cultural institutionalization of certain cultural dimensions among its members do have an impact on the encouragement and facilitation of entrepreneurial activity. The systematic variation in the levels of entrepreneurship across nations, despite similarities in the economical and political contexts, call for a cultural justification. In contrast to other studies that compare and differentiate the cultural value system of entrepreneurs with non-entrepreneurs, this paper looks at the wider macro picture in relating the dominant culture's dimensions that produced such high levels of entrepreneurs and entrepreneurial ventures (without focusing on their prior or current individual value system) – in other words, the "supply side".

Building on the entrepreneurship and culture literature, I propose a number of theoretical arguments and empirical assessments of the association between the relevant cultural dimensions and the levels of entrepreneurial activity across countries. As reviewed in this dissertation, I shall employ the entrepreneurship data from GEM and the culture data and conceptualization from GLOBE. Hence, the following discussion and theorization draws on a large deal from these two sources as well as other literature. The dissertation paper will hypothesize relationships between seven[2] dimensions of national culture drawn from GLOBE (namely: Performance Orientation, Uncertainty Avoidance, Collectivism "two sub-dimensions", Assertiveness, Future Orientation, and Power Distance) and the aggregate national entrepreneurial activity levels drawn from GEM (Early-Stage Total Entrepreneurial Activity – TEA).

---

[2] GLOBE lists two more independent cultural dimensions (Humane Orientation and Gender Egalitarianism). They are not being studied here due to the paper's unavailability of theoretical justification for directly linking them to aggregate levels of entrepreneurship. The choice of the seven other cultural dimensions to be studied in this paper was based on their perceived relevance to entrepreneurship. However, this still remains an opportunity for future research.

3.2.1. Performance Orientation:

The cultural dimension of Performance Orientation, according to GLOBE, is what "reflects the extent to which a community encourages and rewards innovation, high standards, and performance improvement". Regardless of its apparent distinguishing significance, this concept has neither been identified by Hofstede as an independent cultural dimension nor received much attention in the literature (House et al., 2004). However, the Performance Orientation dimension has some overlapping with Hofstede's Masculinity Index, although they do differ in a number of points that may have left Hofstede's Index to be described as confusing in this regard (McGrath, MacMillan, & Scheinberg, 1992). And this is may well be one of the reasons why Wu (2007) failed to find a correlation between Hofstede's Masculinity dimension and the level of entrepreneurial activity. According to Hofstede (2001), masculine societies place greater emphasis on individual achievement and rewards than do feminine societies. Nevertheless, the Performance Orientation dimension does indeed seem to be a historically differentiating cultural factor. According to the classical works of Max Weber, the essence of this dimension is more relevant to the Protestant religious doctrine, which emphasizes the idea of work as a sacred call and a determinant of personal salvation (1904). The Catholic doctrine, on the other hand, focuses more on the humane aspects of good deeds, charity, and maintaining peace as an exclusive path to salvation. The Asian Confucian culture, in the same vein, seems to also coincide with the Protestant doctrine, where it encourages hard work, acquiring new skills, patience, and thrift (Hofstede & Bond, 1988).

Another relevant concept to this dimension is the Need for Achievement (*nAch*), which was initially introduced by McClelland and colleagues (1961; 1987; Brockhaus, 1982; Brockhaus & Horwitz, 1986). It is defined as "the need to do better all the time" (McClelland, 1987), where cultures that promote this spirit tend to support its members' self-confidence, self-reliance, and efforts to set high standards for their success and work hard to achieve their goals. Individuals who possess a high level of this need tend to value work, enjoy progressive improvement, accept personal responsibilities for outcomes, and are generally innovative (McClelland, 1987). These qualities are assumed to be determinant factors for successful initiators of new ventures (Mueller & Thomas, 2000; Gupta et al., 2008) and some are qualities that differentiate entrepreneurs from small business managers (Begley & Boyd, 1987). Hence, it is no surprise that the GLOBE study found that societies which score higher on this dimension tend to expect demanding targets, believe that individuals are in control, value and reward individual achievement, value taking initiative, and believe that anyone can succeed if he/she tries hard; among other tendencies (House et al., 2004) – which are all characteristics commonly associated with a favorable environment for entrepreneurship. The transmittance of such values to new generations could be through education and/or, most importantly, parenthood. This, consequently, leads individuals into becoming active entrepreneurs and economic-value generators (House et al., 2004). The cognition theory literature provides an explanation of this cultural influence. A cultural dimension – like Performance Orientation – is transmitted to the members of a given culture through a shared cognitive schema that dictates an individual's perception of matters or events in life (such as entrepreneurship) and his/her frameworks and structures in dealing with it. Interpretation is subsequently is the stage where such perception is given meaning (e.g. Weick, 1995). Then, individuals make sense of this perception/meaning leading to either embrace or reject it – the "correct thing to do" - based on the individual's identification with a certain group (Morrison & Milliken, 2000; Young & Parker, 1999; Porac et al., 1989). High Performance Orientation cultures possess collective frameworks and structures that promote events that are in line with this dimension (e.g. entrepreneurship as a high-performance activity as discussed above) through the different stages of cognition. Moreover, from an institutional perspective, individuals/organizations draw on the institution's (here: culture) criteria in evaluating its organizational structures and not on their own, possibly efficiency-driven, criteria (Engelen et al., 2009; Scott & Meyer, 1991). Hence, a culture that is high in Performance Orientation will put pressure on its members to share its acceptance (DiMaggion & Powell, 1983) of high-performance activities (such as entrepreneurship); through coercive isomorphism (from their peers) and normative isomorphism (from common education and associations).

Based on the above theorization, I propose that:

H1: The higher a culture's score in Performance Orientation, the higher its National Entrepreneurial Activity.

3.2.2. Uncertainty Avoidance:

According to GLOBE, Uncertainty Avoidance "involves the extent to which ambiguous situations are threatening to individuals, to which rules and order are preferred, and to which uncertainty is tolerated in a society". Uncertainty avoiding cultures tend to rely on norms, rules, and order to "alleviate [the] unpredictability of future events" (House et al., 2004). Hofstede, who also has identified this dimension as an independent variable, defined it as "the extent to which the members of a culture feel threatened by uncertain or unknown situations" (2001). He also argued that strategies for coping with uncertainty are rooted in culture and reinforced through basic institutions such as family, school, and state, (Hofstede, 2001; Mueller & Thomas, 2000).

This concept has been originally used by Cyert & March (1963 – cited in House et al., 2004) and later populated after Hofstede's Culture's Consequences book suggested its cultural-level variability (Ribchester, 1995 - cited in Hofstede, 2001). Societies have adapted to this uncertainty in many ways. These different ways do not only differ between traditional and modern societies, but also among modern societies (Hofstede, 2001). We should note, however, that this concept should not be confused with "risk avoidance" in, for example, business decisions. Risk avoidance and uncertainty avoidance are two different concepts; where "uncertainty is to risk as anxiety to fear" (Hofstede, 2001). If uncertainty becomes quantified – as in the case of risk, it ceases to be anxious to its beholder. Uncertainty avoidance aims to escape from ambiguity, not risk. Uncertainty avoidant cultures seem to search for order, norms, and institutions that make things more predictable. Technology, law, and religion are believed to be aiding mechanisms that help high uncertainty avoiding cultures cope with ambiguity (House et al., 2004; Hofstede, 2001). However, both GLOBE and Hofstede's studies advance that such phenomenon is meant to describe and represent the culture level of analysis. Hence, it shouldn't be very apparent or applicable at the individual level. Applying its face value to the individual level may fall in both what is termed "ecological fallacy" and "reductionism". This questions the validity of the numerous published studies that correlate this and other concepts to the individual level.

In both GLOBE and Hofstede studies, low uncertainty avoidance cultures (relevant to high uncertainty avoidance cultures) tend to be informal in the interactions of its members, less concerned with orderliness, encouraging new product development and innovation, show less resistance to change, facilitate the change of employers (employment mobility), and show more tolerance for breaking rules. These cultural characteristics translate in an environment where entrepreneurship could flourish and even be encouraged. This is in line with the findings that show entrepreneurs to normally behave in a confident and wishful way (Bernardo & Welch, 2001; Cooper, Woo and Dunkelberg 1988), where they show a fair understanding of the present but have rather special views regarding the future (Licht & Siegel, 2005). They have also been found to be over optimistic and under-estimating the risks associated with the unknown (Palich & Babgy 1995; Sarasvathy, Simon & Lave 1998).

Another related concept is the "Locus of Control", which was repeatedly associated with entrepreneurship in the literature (e.g. Bird, 1989; Mueller et al., 2002). Rotter (1966), who has been credited for developing this concept, advances that an "internal locus of control" individual believes that the future can be controlled through one's effort (Gupta & Fernandez, 2009) by his/her ability, struggle, or skills (Mueller & Thomas, 2000). On the other hand, an "external locus of control" individual believes that forces outside the control of humans determine outcomes. The logic of accepting ambiguity and projecting a confident control of outcomes seems to be common in both this concept and the low uncertainty avoiding cultures. And this mode of thinking best resembles the state of the entrepreneur (Brockhaus 1982; Brockhaus and Horowitz 1986; McGrath, MacMillan, & Scheinberg, 1992), where the entrepreneurial process is believed to be full of uncertainty and challenges (e.g. Amit, Glosten, & Muller, 1993). In low uncertainty avoidance cultures, the social deviants (such as the entrepreneur) are not perceived as threatening or dangerous, instead; there is more willingness to take risks, and achievement is often recognized as a pioneering effort (Hofstede 1980, Steensma et al., 2000). In contrast, high uncertainty avoidance cultures tend to have a great resistance and fear towards failure, a lower willingness to take risks, lower levels of ambition, tight organizational structures, specialized career paths, and lower tolerance of ambiguity (Hofstede, 2001). These tendencies are believed to be incompatible with the entrepreneurial setting (Busenitz & Lau, 1997).

In the same vein, Shane (1993) found that cultures with low uncertainty avoidance levels enjoy high rates of national innovation. This is in line with the argument that low uncertainty avoidance implies a greater willingness to enter into unknown ventures (Hofstede, 2001). And since low uncertainty avoidance cultures have a more facilitating environment for "deviant" behaviors, this implies that entrepreneurial actions in these cultures enjoy more freedom and legitimacy than in high uncertainty avoidance cultures (Mueller & Thomas, 2000; Mueller et al., 2002). This is coined in the institutional theory by the "social stimuli" (DiMaggio & Powell, 1983; Meyer & Rowan, 1977; Scott, 1995; Scott, 2005); where culture shapes the undertaken actions by its members. Failing to live with such legitimizing rules and norms will lead organizations/individuals to die off, or at least, be perceived as deviants. Hence, facets of cultures – such as high Uncertainty Avoidance – institutionalizes the evaluation criteria of accepting/rejecting cultural activities or behaviors (e.g. entrepreneurship).

Based on this, I propose that:.

H2: The higher a culture's score in Uncertainty Avoidance, the lower its National Entrepreneurial Activity.

3.2.3. Collectivism:

The concept of collectivism/individualism has been one of the most debated and discussed notions in the literature since very early times (Hofstede, 2001; House et al., 2004). Various early and contemporary authors have recognized it as a distinguishing cultural variable among societies in the world (e.g. Parsons, 1949). Hofstede's last publications (e.g. 2001) cover this dimension and they have a great influence on its popularity in the field of management research. As defined by him, individualism characterizes "societies in which the ties between individuals are loose: everyone is expected to look after himself/herself and his/her immediate family. Collectivism, as its opposite, pertains to societies in which people from birth onwards are integrated into strong, cohesive in-groups, which throughout people's lifetime continue to protect them in exchange for unquestioning loyalty" (Hofstede, 1991).

Most of the entrepreneurship literature has fiercely associated individualist cultures with entrepreneurship (e.g. Mitchell et al., 2000; McGrath, MacMillan, & Scheinberg, 1992). They have linked the characteristics prevalent in individualistic cultures, such as independence, free career mobility, self-reliance, etc., to the traits of entrepreneurs in the literature. Some have even argued that the individualistic society is by definition an entrepreneurial society (McClelland, 1961). However, another block of researchers, when empirically testing this association, have found either no proof (e.g. Mueller et al., 2002) or a totally counter finding that shows individualism as having a *negative* impact on the national levels of entrepreneurship (Wu, 2007; Baum, Olian, Erez, Schnell, Smith, Sims, Scully, & Smith, 1993). Another study on Nepalese entrepreneurs found that successful ones seem to possess qualities that are associated with *both* individualism and collectivism (Bhawuk & Udas, 1996). This contradiction of findings and arguments call for a better theoretical explanation of the link between this popular, yet un-agreed-upon, construct and entrepreneurship.

I argue that this paradox of contradicting findings could mainly be traced to the explanation of the collectivism/individualism dimension. As the most prevalent source of definition and classification, Hofstede's conceptualization of this dimension seems to have two main problems in this regard: 1) It confuses values and practices, and 2) It treats two underlying systems as one. By two underlying systems I mean that collectivism constitutes two dimensions; *horizontal* and *vertical*. As the pioneer of this view, Triandis (1995) advanced that the most important attributes that distinguish among different kinds of individualism and collectivism are the relative emphasis on horizontal and vertical social relationships. Horizontal relationships assume that one self is more or less like every other self. One the other hand, vertical relationships consist of hierarchies, and one self is rather different from other selves (House et al., 2004). The GLOBE Study has built upon such conceptualization through the development of two unique constructs studied at the societal level. This has resulted in developing two unique measures; namely, *Institutional Collectivism* and *In-Group Collectivism*. I argue that these two measures, which I shall discuss separately in the next sections, capture two theoretically different aspects that have two different implications on entrepreneurship; one negative/hindering and the other positive/encouraging.

3.2.3.1. Institutional Collectivism:

Institutional Collectivism is defined as "the degree to which organizational and societal institutional practices encourage and reward collective distribution of resources and collective action" (House et al., 2004). The GLOBE authors further advance that this dimension's question items were aimed to assess "whether group loyalty is emphasized at the expense of individual goals, whether the economic system emphasizes individual or collective interests, whether being accepted by other group members is important, and whether individualism or group cohesion is valued more in the society". Hence, I argue that this dimension more clearly reflects the dysfunctional/hindering pressure that a society can play against entrepreneurial activities and individuals. It stresses upon the collective rewards and distribution of resources over individual gains and goals; which contradicts the essence of venture creation as an individual action for a self gain over competition.

This tendency is, to some extent, in line with the Asian Confucian philosophy, where individuals are regarded as relatively unimportant and that societies are comprised of families, not individuals (Redding, 1990). The word "man" has even a very different meaning in Chinese than in English (Lockett, 1987), where it constitutes of a web of relationships that individuals identify themselves with. This is also in line with the "theory of face", most commonly prevalent in Asian cultures (e.g. Begley & Tan, 2001). In order to protect one's "loss of face" in such cultures, members tend to value the harmony and cohesiveness of their actions with the society, which enforces a stricter alignment of individual interests with the societal ones. I argue that this is the underlying system that most commonly referred to in the literature as disadvantageous to entrepreneurship (e.g. Sexton & Bowman, 1985; McGrath, MacMillan, Scheinberg, 1992; Hayton et al., 2002); as it undervalues the interests and rewards of individual venture-creators for the sake of the collective good. The Need for Autonomy (*nAut*) and independence, as discussed widely in literature, contradicts such cultural value (Brockhaus, 1982; Brockhaus & Horwitz, 1986; McGrath, MacMillan, Scheinberg, 1992). The literature widely confirms that entrepreneurs give special importance to their independence (Sexton & Bowman, 1985; Blanchflower & Oswald 1998; Blanchflower 2000; Hundley 2001). Hence, the perception of entrepreneurship could be assumed to be unacceptable/resisted in cultures with high Institutional Collectivism. This reflects the pressures played by the institutional isomorphism in sharing the resistance/detest of entrepreneurship. This also - borrowing from the cognitive thread of research - means that the shared cognitive schema of a given culture that is high in institutional collectivism restricts its members efforts to make sense of events to the collectively-acceptable norms; which in turn reflect negatively on the aggregate levels of entrepreneurship.

And based on the above, I propose that:

H3: The higher a culture's score in Institutional Collectivism, the lower its National Entrepreneurial Activity.

3.2.3.2. In-Group Collectivism:

Rather than focusing on the societal goals as taking priority over individual goals, the In-Group Collectivism dimension looks at culture from a different point of view. It is defined as "the degree to which individuals express pride, loyalty, and cohesiveness in their organizations and families" (House et al., 2004). This construct was operationalized using question items that measured "whether children take pride in the individual accomplishments of their parents and vice versa, whether aging parents live at home with their children, and whether children live at home with their parents until they get married". This dimension, therefore, measured for the inter-reliance and dependability of small group (e.g. family) members on each other; as a society-level value and practice. In contrast to the Institutional Collectivism, this dimension stresses on the reliance of people on each other without discounting their own individual ambitions and goals.

I argue that the elements of this dimension are very much aligned with the arguments that highlight the importance of certain group/ collective mechanisms in the success of entrepreneurial ventures. The literature discusses the role of networks as an essential and facilitating factor for entrepreneurship (Gompers, Lerner, & Scharfstein, 2005; Licht & Siegel, 2005). Brüderal & Preisendörfer (1998), in their network success hypothesis, argue that it has been commonly accepted that "those entrepreneurs who can refer to a broad and diverse social network and who receive much support from their network are more successful". In other words, such web of trustworthy network members (through family and friends) could offer the entrepreneur a large deal of resources and assistance in the recognition of opportunities, structuring of venture, and maintenance of performance that otherwise would not be available (Birley, 1985; Aldrich & Zimmer, 1986; Aldrich & Cliff, 2003). In the same vein, Portes & Sensenbrenner (1993) describe how entrepreneurs acquire their social capital in an aim to gain trust of their "network". They advance that there are four sources of capital; 1) *value introjection*, which is "based on identity from birth with a group, and leads the individual to behave in altruistic ways specifically towards members of that group"; 2) *reciprocity exchan*ges, which "leads individuals to act generously to others in a defined group based on an established norm of reciprocity"; 3) *bounded solidarity*, "which comes from having experiences a common event or set of events during the course of life with a defined group of people"; and finally 4) *enforceable trust*, which "comes from an expectation that a defined group would punish any individual who treats another member of the group inappropriately" (Licht & Siegel, 2005). The first two sources seem to be the most related concepts to the role of networks in the success or failure of entrepreneurs in the society. Cultures that enjoy a high level of in-group collectivism (or network strength and reach) offer such aiding resources for its members in exchange for their loyalty and pride. In contrast to the previous sub-dimension, the essence of In-Group Collectivism is strongly aligned with entrepreneurship. And through the same cognitive filtration frameworks and institutional pressures and restrictions, entrepreneurship will be a welcomed behavior in high In-Group Collectivism cultures.

The confusion of mixing the elements of both Institutional Collectivism and In-Group Collectivism, and the adoption of a general and inadequate theorization that does not identify and differentiate between these two distinct manifestations of the term "collectivism" are the main reasons for the conflicting and contradicting results in the literature. This dissertation paper intends to appropriately differentiate between the two seemingly-similar but theoretically-different constructs by highlighting their negative and positive correlations with entrepreneurship.

Based on the above theorization, I propose that:

H4: The higher a culture's score in In-Group Collectivism, the higher its National Entrepreneurial Activity.

3.2.4. Assertiveness:

According to GLOBE, the Assertiveness dimension is defined as "the degree to which individuals in organizations or societies are assertive, tough, dominant, and aggressive in social relationships" (House et al., 2004). The dimension was meant to measure "whether people are or should be encouraged to be assertive, aggressive, and tough; or nonassertive, nonaggressive, and tender in social relationships". Webster's dictionary, also, defines the term "assertive" as "positive or confident in a persistence way". The dictionary also lists "aggressive" as one synonym, where one of its definitions is "enterprising or taking initiative". Despite this dimension's importance in distinguishing behaviors in societies and its common connotations to business, it has received very little attention in the literature (House et al., 2004). The assertive behavior has been widely resembled as a successful business trait, where projections of this could be seen in Nike's "Just do it" slogan and the industry's popular terminologies such as "aggressive marketing strategies" (House et al., 2004).

However, the origins of this GLOBE dimension stems partially from Hofstede's Masculinity Index. Despite the fact that Hofstede's masculinity dimension carries some elements of this dimension, it is not quite the same. One difference is that Hofstede's dimension confounds gender inequality with success striving in the same measure, which are two issues not necessarily correlated. Another difference is the failure of Hofstede's dimension in directly measuring assertiveness. Being performance-oriented does not necessarily mean assertive (House et al., 2004). Hence, this leaves the Masculinity Index to be confused with many societal values and cultural dimensions such as the Humane Orientation, Performance Orientation, Assertiveness, and Gender Egalitarianism.

The literature discusses the "assertive behavior", where it was contrasted with the "passive behavior" (Crawford, 1995). Passive behavior is attributed to "those who fail to express their true thoughts and feelings, allow themselves to be dominated or humiliated by others, and who comply with requests or demands of others even if they themselves do not want to" (Lange & Jabuwkoski, 1976). The assertive behavior has been associated with successful managers (e.g. Brenner, Tomkiewicz, & Schein, 1989; House et al., 2004), regardless of the gender of who possess it (Fagenson, 1990). Culture constitutes one of the contextual influences that legitimizes the adoption and acceptance of certain behaviors among its members; such as assertiveness (Rakos, 1991). A culture high in assertiveness can resemble what is termed a "doing" orientation; where the individual is believed to be able to take charge and actively control the environment around him/her. This is in contrast to the "being" orientation, where fatalism prevails. Under this "being" notion, humans are just observant of the powerful nature (Kluckhohn & Strodbeck, 1961). The highly assertive (and "doing") cultures are expected to believe in the value of competition and competitiveness, in line with the popular terms of "Eat or be eaten" or "Control your destiny" (House et al., 2004). In their review, Doney, Cannon, & Mullen (1998) note that the culture with high assertiveness tend to believe in opportunism. In such cultures, the potential rewards for an opportunistic behavior seems to overweigh its costs.

With regards to the entrepreneurship literature, this dimension has a lot in common with the Need for Achievement - which we previously discussed – where the entrepreneur is depicted as someone who preferred to take responsibility for decisions and set goals and accomplish them through his own effort (McClelland, 1961). Despite the potential monetary and financial gain present in entrepreneurial ventures (as in the focus of Performance Orientation, for example), the identification of potentially good opportunity requires a behavior to act upon it. Accordingly, Shane & Venkataraman's (2000) Discovery, Evaluation and Exploitation (DEE) framework imply that entrepreneurs should be able to "exploit" the perceived opportunities. This exploitation will not materialize under a submissive "passive" behavior. Marshalling resources, patience, and sticking to one's goals are all aspects of assertiveness. In this vein, a number of entrepreneurial traits and values can be observed in the tendencies of high-assertiveness societies. GLOBE lists a number of tendencies that include: valuing competition, valuing success and progress, trying to have control over the environment, having a "can-do" attitude, valuing the take of initiative, and acting and thinking of others in an opportunistic way. Hence, we can see a rational link between the assertiveness of a culture and its encouragement and acceptance of assertive manifestations, such as the entrepreneurial decision and action. Given this inherited endorsement of entrepreneurial behaviors in highly assertive cultures, it is expected that such culture puts an institutional pressure among its members to embrace entrepreneurship; through coercive and normative isomorphism in order to gain external legitimacy. The cognitive thread of research also supports this tendency through the society's shaping of one's interpretation and subsequent sensemaking of events.

Based on this theorization, I propose:

H5: The higher a culture's score in Assertiveness, the higher its National Entrepreneurial Activity.

3.2.5. *Future Orientation:*

The Future Orientation dimension is defined by GLOBE as "the extent to which individuals engage in future-oriented behaviors such as delaying gratification, planning, and investing in the future". It is the "degree to which a collectivity encourages and rewards future-oriented behaviors such as planning and delaying gratification" (House et al., 2004). Labeled as one of the most fundamental aspects of culture (Bluedorn, 2000), the Future Orientation concept has been heavily covered in the literature (House et al., 2004) using various schemes to interpret and operationalize it (Seijts, 1998). The first traced categorization of time into three classifications (e.g. past orientation, present orientation, and future orientation) has been credited to Lewin (1942 - cited in House et al., 2004), who ignited the consequential adoption of this classification in the fields of management, psychology, and cross-cultural research. The increasing interest in the "future-orientation" has emerged due to its association with progress, innovation, and achievement (Teather & Chow, 2000). The future or time became regarded as a commodity and an equivalent to money; best resembled in the popular term "save time" (Becker, 1965). Cultures with low future orientation tend to focus on enjoying the moment and be spontaneous. But this leads also to the incapacity or unwillingness to plan a sequence to realize their desired goals. On the other hand, cultures with high future orientation possess a solid capability and interest in envisioning future contingencies, develop future goals, and seek to achieve such goals through practical strategies (House et al., 2004; Keough, Zimbardo, & Boyd, 1999). This has lead GLOBE to characterize the future-oriented culture as the one with members who "... believe that their current actions will influence their future, focus on investment in their future, believe that they will have a future that matters, believe in planning for developing their future, and look far into the future for assessing the effects of their current actions" (House et al., 2004).

Many managerial aspects and processes seem to rely on the acknowledgment and instrumentality of the Future Orientation dimension, which include: strategy development (Trompenaars & Hampden-Turner, 1998), planning (Ansoff, 1988), organizational and managerial flexibility (Tendam, 1987), and even depicting it as a predictor of better organizational performance (Schriber & Gutek, 1987). However, despite its apparent relevance to entrepreneurship and venture creation, the literature seems to have no paper that empirically links this dimension to aggregate entrepreneurship. For example, Busenitz & Lau (1997) proposed to link it to the entrepreneurial *cognition* at the *individual level*, without actually testing it. Moreover, in his study on Sub Saharan Africa, Takyi-Asiedu (1993) linked Confucian Dynamism (which is not quite the same as Future Orientation, but may compose some aspects of it) to entrepreneurship. According to GLOBE, cultures that score high in Future Orientation tend to: achieve economic success, have individuals who are more intrinsically motivated, have a longer strategies orientation, have flexible and adaptive organizations and managers, and place a higher priority on long-term success and deference of gratification/

rewards (House et al., 2004). All of these tendencies seem to be in line with the field's depiction of a facilitating environment for entrepreneurship. Entrepreneurship, as an organized and future-dependent process, could very well be associated with Future Orientation. The fact that new ventures require a great deal of patience, support, planning, strategies, and flexibility to materialize provides a solid link to this cultural dimension. Therefore, cultures, in essence, institutionalizes Future Orientation as the "legitimate" framework and evaluation criteria for its members; leading them to embrace activities (such as entrepreneurship) that are aligned with it. This is transmitted through the collective cognitive schema, interpretation, and sensemaking phases of observing and processing events around people.

Based on this, I propose:

H6: The higher a culture's score in Future Orientation, the higher its National Entrepreneurial Activity.

3.2.6. Power Distance:

In defining Power Distance, GLOBE states that it is "the degree to which members of an organization or society expect and agree that power should be unequally shared". It resembles the "extent to which a community accepts and endorses authority, power differences, and status privileges" (House et al., 2004). Mulder is among the first to use the term of power distance, where he characterized it as "the degree of inequality in power between a less powerful Individual ('I') and a more powerful Other ('O'), in which 'I' and 'O' belong to the same - loosely or tightly knit - social system" (Mulder, 1977). Building on this, Hofstede argued that "the basic issue involved … is [the] human equality. Inequality can occur in areas such as prestige, wealth, and power; and different societies put different weights on status consistency among these areas" (Hofstede, 2001). In other words, a culture of high power distance is the one which accepts power concentration. This is in contrast to cultures with low power distance, which believe in power decentralization. However, lets first question the justification for an individual with an inherit need for power in a high power distance culture to submit to another individual's power and control over him/her. This can mainly be traced to the individual's prioritization of needs. For instance, keeping a job in a firm, despite the superiors' pressures and control, may constitutes a higher priority to this individual than leaving the firm and having ultimate power over his/her destiny (House et al., 2004). This preference for a state of hierarchal order and leadership could be a shared societal value, where the unequal distribution of power is tolerated and embraced.

High power distance countries, such as New Zealand, would have individuals (or elites) who are perceived to have a higher rank and power that is beyond the reach of the rest. Such rank and power may be due to their expertise or referent power (French & Raven, 1959). On the other hand, countries with a low power distance, such as the Netherland, would have relatively equal opportunities for its members to access the varying classes and jobs based on a mutual respect and appreciation to each one's contribution and knowledge. Their main basis for such treatment is the detest of mere power, where it is assumed to be a corrupting factor (House et al., 2004). GLOBE also traced the main drivers of accepting or rejecting the equal power distribution in societies to: the predominant religion, the tradition of democratic principles of government, the existence of a strong middle class, and the proportion of immigrants in a society's population. Countries with high power distance, according to GLOBE and Hofstede (2001) tend to have a stable and concentrated power, limited social and occupational mobility, strong hierarchical organizations, protected non-shared information, wide salary range between top and bottom of organizations, and relatively few individuals with access to resources, skills, and capabilities.

However, the entrepreneurship literature seems to be in a state of flux with regards to this dimension's impact on entrepreneurship. After reviewing the literature, there seems to be two contradicting threads of arguments. On the one hand, some researchers argue that in order for entrepreneurship to flourish, there has to be a relatively low societal level of power distance. In such culture, information is exchanged freely, people have equal rights and opportunities, and democratic decision-making is valued. All these values have been argued to support a healthy environment for the creation of ventures. In this vein, Shane (1992; 1993), although not directly addressing the issue of entrepreneurship, found that power distance is negatively correlated with national innovation. He reasoned this to the propensity of innovation to require a free, open, and information-sharing environment, which is best resembled in a low power distance culture. Along the same lines and using the idea of social mobility restrictions, Mueller et al. (2002) also hypothesized the same relationship of this dimension with potential entrepreneurs; although his hypothesis was not supported. Wu (2007) used the need for autonomy and independence arguments to also propose an association between low power distance and high levels of entrepreneurship (hypothesis not supported). In his studies of cognition and the entrepreneurial decision-making, Mitchell et al. (2000) have also advanced the idea that in high power distance countries, the small elite group of people controls the access to resources and skills necessary for identifying opportunities and acting upon them. The rest of population, who are at lower classes, may find entrepreneurial activities as something only the elite do. They also, most probably, do not have the resources to take advantage of opportunities.

On the other hand, another analysis suggests the opposite (McGrath, MacMillan, & Scheinberg, 1992; Verheul et al., 2002; Wildeman, Hofstede, Noorderhaven, Thurik, Verhoeven, & Wennekers, 1999), where the argument is that entrepreneurship may best be found in high power distance cultures. One justification for this claim is that entrepreneurs are believed to be individuals who attempt to catch up with others in society from a position of disadvantage (Brenner, 1987). Therefore, in a culture that portrays inequality (high power distance), the need for "catching up" will be escalated. Entrepreneurs will compensate their inherited disadvantage by being their own bosses in an aim to reach a "higher position" (McGrath, MacMillan, & Scheinberg, 1992). This is coined in the literature with the arguments that suggest entrepreneurs cannot accept authority (Hagen, 1962). This idea counters the first camp's expectation of low entrepreneurship when there inequality and limited access to resources. Instead of this reality being a constant constraint (see above argument – e.g. Mitchell et al., 2000), it actually triggers a strong human need to overcome it; i.e. catch up. Another justification for this link could be found in the argument that individuals decide to be entrepreneurs because of their *dissatisfaction* with the status quo. Since it has been found that the negative previous work experiences that individuals face constitute a major factor for influencing their decision to start a new business (Collins, Moore, & Unwalla, 1964; Shapero, 1975), researchers have argued that a culture of high inequality, suppressive nature, and wide salary differences (high power distance) will create particular incentives for starting a new business and a source of entrepreneurship (Verheul et al., 2002; MacGrath, MacMillan, & Scheinberg, 1992; Wildeman et al., 1999). Hence, based on this and on the arguments that take into account the motivating drivers behind the entrepreneurs' bold move (i.e. need to catch up, dissatisfaction with suppression and inequality), it could be assumed that cultures with high Power Distance would accept and encourage entrepreneurship. The process of such acceptance/encouragement is practiced through the limitation imposed by the collective cognitive schema that gives meaning and sense to events. It is also practiced through the institutional pressures imposed by peers and the wide culture.

Based on the above, I propose:

H7: The higher a culture's score in Power Distance, the higher its National Entrepreneurship Activity.

4. METHODOLOGY

The sample of this study consists of 244 observations, from 51 countries (in six continents), across 8 years (2004-2011). The choice of countries was based on and limited by the availability of matched data from the two global projects; GEM and GLOBE. This compiled pool of data is significantly large compared to other similar studies. This is due to the known financial and logistical challenges faced by any researcher in acquiring comparable, country-level data of this nature.

The level of analysis is strictly the country. Hence, the data represent the aggregate, country-level scores. Any findings or judgments in this level of analysis should not be assumed to be true for other levels of analysis; e.g. the individual level. Failing to recognize this leads to falling into what was termed "ecological fallacy" (Hofstede, 1980; 2001).

The two main constructs to be measured are national entrepreneurship (the dependent variable) and national culture (the independent variable). National entrepreneurship is operationalized using the measure of Early-Stage Total Entrepreneurial Activity (TEA), which is obtained from the findings of the Global Entrepreneurship Monitor (GEM) in the year range of 2004-2011. The GEM data offers researchers the possibility to assess the rates of entrepreneurial activity in a comparable, cross-country manner. More information about this project and data can be found in the review of measurements at the Literature Review section of this dissertation. The TEA score (Early-Stage Total Entrepreneurial Activity) is defined as the "the proportion of people aged 18-64 who are involved in entrepreneurial activity as a nascent entrepreneur or as an owner-manager of a new business" (GEM Executive Report 2009). It is important to note that the GEM project measures entrepreneurial activity levels directly through the responses of sampled adult individuals, not through secondary data or government records. The below table illustrates each country's score of TEA across the years; where score numbers are percentages of the total population of the country. Note that some countries are absent from some years due to the non-participation of their national teams.

After calculating the averages of each country's TEA scores within the year range (2004-2011), it could be noticed that the following countries scored the highest: Nigeria (34.99), Bolivia (34.21), Zambia (32.63), Colombia (22.39), and Thailand (20.58). On the other hand, the following countries scored the lowest averages: Japan (3.52), Austria (3.86), Russia (3.90), Italy (4.06), and Sweden (3.43). Moreover, when analyzing the year averages (average of all country scores in each year), it could be noticed that the trend reflects the global economic situation. The year of 2008 has widely been recognized as the inception period for the tragic economic slowdown. The TEA data echoes this; where average scores where increasing from 2004 up to a peak in 2008. The following year – 2009 – saw a drop (around 5.7% from 2008 average) that quickly picked up afterwards to a record-high in 2011 (10.66).

Table 1

		TEA (GEM)							
		2004	2005	2006	2007	2008	2009	2010	2011
1	Argentina	12.84	9.49	10.24	14.43	16.54	14.68	14.2	20.78
2	Australia	13.38	10.87	11.96				7.8	10.5
3	Austria		5.28		2.44				
4	Bolivia					29.82		38.6	
5	Brazil	13.48	11.32	11.65	12.72	12.02	15.32	17.5	14.89
6	Canada	8.85	9.33	7.12					
7	China		13.72	16.19	16.43		18.84	14.37	24.01
8	Colombia			22.48	22.72	24.52	22.57	20.61	21.44
9	Costa Rica							13.44	
10	Denmark	5.31	4.75	5.32	5.39	4.44	3.64	3.77	4.63
11	Ecuador	27.24				17.18	15.82	21.25	
12	Egypt					13.11		7.02	
13	England	6.25	6.22	5.77	5.53	5.91	5.74	6.42	7.29
14	Finland	4.39	4.97	4.99	6.91	7.34	5.17	5.72	6.25
15	France	6.03	5.35	4.39	3.17	5.64	4.35	5.83	5.73
16	Germany	5.07	5.39	4.21		3.77	4.1	4.17	5.62
17	Greece	5.77	6.5	7.9	5.71	9.86	8.79	5.51	7.95
18	Guatemala						19.2	16.3	19.31
19	Hong Kong	2.97			9.95		3.64		
20	Hungary	4.29	1.9	6.04	6.86	6.61	9.13	7.13	6.29
21	India			10.42	8.53	11.49			
22	Indonesia			19.28					
23	Iran					9.18	12.08	12.31	14.54
24	Ireland	7.7	9.83	7.35	8.22	7.59		6.76	7.25
25	Israel	6.62			5.44	6.45	6.07	5.02	
26	Italy	4.32	4.94	3.47	5.01	4.62	3.72	2.35	
27	Japan	1.48	2.2	2.9	4.34	5.42	3.26	3.3	5.22
28	Kazakhstan				9.36				
29	Malaysia			11.09			4.41	4.96	4.92
30	Mexico		5.91	5.26		13.09		10.45	9.62
31	Morocco						15.75		

32	Netherlands	5.11	4.36	5.42	5.18	5.2	7.19	7.22	8.21
33	New Zealand	14.67	17.57						
34	Nigeria								34.99
35	Philippines			20.44					
36	Poland	8.83							9.03
37	Portugal	3.95			8.78			4.4	7.54
38	Russia			4.86	2.67	3.49	3.88	3.94	4.57
39	Singapore	5.69	7.24	4.85					6.6
40	Slovenia	2.6	4.36	4.63	4.78	6.4	5.36	4.65	3.65
41	South Africa	5.4	5.15	5.29		7.76	5.92	8.86	9.14
42	South Korea					9.99	7.01	6.56	7.82
43	Spain	5.15	5.65	7.27	7.62	7.03	5.1	4.31	5.81
44	Sweden	3.71	4.04	3.45	4.15			4.88	5.8
45	Switzerland		6.06		6.27		7.72	5.04	6.58
46	Taiwan							8.37	7.91
47	Thailand		20.74	15.2	26.87				19.51
48	Turkey			6.07	5.58	5.96		8.59	11.87
49	United States	11.33	12.44	10.03	9.61	10.76	7.96	7.59	12.34
50	Venezuela		25		20.16		18.66		15.43
51	Zambia							32.63	

National culture, on the other hand, is operationalized using different cultural dimensions obtained from the GLOBE study (Global Leadership and Organizational Behavior Effectiveness Research Program). Namely, these constructs are: Performance Orientation, Uncertainty Avoidance, Institutional Collectivism, In-Group Collectivism, Assertiveness, Future Orientation, and Power Distance. More information about this project can also be found in the Literature Review. The GLOBE study measures two aspects of each cultural dimension; i.e. values (the "should be") and practices (the "as is"). Due to the nature of this dissertation and the practical action of entrepreneurship, the focus here will be on the "practices" aspect of the cultural dimensions. Practices are the realistic perceptions of individuals on what is actually happening in their respective cultures; which is a more relevant concept to this study and the practical process and action of entrepreneurship. On the other hand, Values are the individuals' perception of what the reality hopefully or should be. The below table illustrates each country's aggregate-level score in the seven dimensions studied in this dissertation. The score figures are aggregates of the sample's responses on a seven-point scale.

A brief synopsis of the highest and lowest country scores for each cultural dimension:

- *Performance Orientation:*

   Highest (Singapore, Hong Kong). Lowest (Greece, Venezuela).

- *Uncertainty Avoidance:*

   Highest (Sweden, Singapore). Lowest (Russia, Hungary).

- *Institutional Collectivism:*

   Highest (Sweden, South Korea). Lowest (Greece, Hungary).

- *In-Group Collectivism:*

   Highest (Philippines, Iran). Lowest (Denmark, Sweden).

- *Assertiveness:*

   Highest (Nigeria, Hungary). Lowest (Sweden, New Zealand).

— *Future Orientation:*

Highest (Singapore, Netherlands). Lowest (Russia, Argentina).

— *Power Distance:*

Highest (Nigeria, Morocco). Lowest (Denmark, Netherlands).

The country of Sweden seems to be the one with most presence in the above brief analysis (whether highest or lowest). This, in turn, tells us that it could be among the most distinct cultures in today's world.

Table 2

		Cultural Dimensions (GLOBE)						
		Performance Orientation	Uncertainty Avoidance	Institutional Collectivism	In-Group Collectivism	Assertiveness	Future Orientation	Power Distance
1	Argentina	3.65	3.65	3.66	5.51	4.22	3.08	5.64
2	Australia	4.36	4.39	4.29	4.17	4.28	4.09	4.74
3	Austria	4.44	5.16	4.3	4.85	4.62	4.46	4.95
4	Bolivia	3.61	3.35	4.04	5.47	3.79	3.61	4.51
5	Brazil	4.04	3.6	3.83	5.18	4.2	3.81	5.33
6	Canada	4.49	4.58	4.38	4.26	4.05	4.44	4.82
7	China	4.45	4.94	4.77	5.8	3.76	3.75	5.04
8	Colombia	3.94	3.57	3.81	5.73	4.2	3.27	5.56
9	Costa Rica	4.12	3.82	3.93	5.32	3.75	3.6	4.74
10	Denmark	4.22	5.22	4.8	3.53	3.8	4.44	3.89
11	Ecuador	4.2	3.68	3.9	5.81	4.09	3.74	5.6

12	Egypt	4.27	4.06	4.5	5.64	3.91	3.86	4.92
13	England	4.08	4.65	4.27	4.08	4.15	4.28	5.15
14	Finland	3.81	5.02	4.63	4.07	3.81	4.24	4.89
15	France	4.11	4.43	3.93	4.37	4.13	3.48	5.28
16	Germany	4.17	5.19	3.675	4.27	4.64	4.11	5.395
17	Greece	3.2	3.39	3.25	5.27	4.58	3.4	5.4
18	Guatemala	3.81	3.3	3.7	5.63	3.89	3.24	5.6
19	Hong Kong	4.8	4.32	4.13	5.32	4.67	4.03	4.96
20	Hungary	3.43	3.12	3.53	5.25	4.79	3.21	5.56
21	India	4.25	4.15	4.38	5.92	3.73	4.19	5.47
22	Indonesia	4.41	4.17	4.54	5.68	3.86	3.86	5.18
23	Iran	4.58	3.67	3.88	6.03	4.04	3.7	5.43
24	Ireland	4.36	4.3	4.63	5.14	3.92	3.98	5.15
25	Israel	4.08	4.01	4.46	4.7	4.23	3.85	4.73
26	Italy	3.58	3.79	3.68	4.94	4.07	3.25	5.43
27	Japan	4.22	4.07	5.19	4.63	3.59	4.29	5.11
28	Kazakhstan	3.57	3.66	4.29	5.26	4.46	3.57	5.31
29	Malaysia	4.34	4.78	4.61	5.51	3.87	4.58	5.17
30	Mexico	4.1	4.18	4.06	5.71	4.45	3.87	5.22
31	Morocco	3.99	3.65	3.87	5.87	4.52	3.26	5.8
32	Netherlands	4.32	4.7	4.46	3.7	4.32	4.61	4.11
33	New Zealand	4.72	4.75	4.81	3.67	3.42	3.47	4.89
34	Nigeria	3.92	4.29	4.14	5.55	4.79	4.09	5.8
35	Philippines	4.47	3.89	4.65	6.36	4.01	4.15	5.44
36	Poland	3.89	3.62	4.53	5.52	4.06	3.11	5.1
37	Portugal	3.6	3.91	3.92	5.51	3.65	3.71	5.44
38	Russia	3.39	2.88	4.5	5.63	3.68	2.88	5.52
39	Singapore	4.9	5.31	4.9	5.64	4.17	5.07	4.99
40	Slovenia	3.66	3.78	4.13	5.43	4	3.59	5.33
41	South Africa	4.385	4.34	4.505	4.795	4.48	4.385	4.635
42	South Korea	4.55	3.55	5.2	5.54	4.4	3.97	5.61
43	Spain	4.01	3.97	3.85	5.45	4.42	3.51	5.52
44	Sweden	3.72	5.32	5.22	3.66	3.38	4.39	4.85
45	Switzerland	4.595	5.175	4.14	3.91	3.99	4.5	4.88
46	Taiwan	4.56	4.34	4.59	5.59	3.92	3.96	5.18

47	Thailand	3.93	3.93	4.03	5.7	3.64	3.43	5.63
48	Turkey	3.83	3.63	4.03	5.88	4.53	3.74	5.57
49	United States	4.49	4.15	4.2	4.25	4.55	4.15	4.88
50	Venezuela	3.32	3.44	3.96	5.53	4.33	3.35	5.4
51	Zambia	4.16	4.1	4.61	5.84	4.07	3.62	5.31

The total available number of countries that can be matched from the above two databases is 51, resulting in 244 data points across 8 years. The following minor tunings have been carried out in order to better match the country-level scores across the two databases - specifically:

– Germany had two separate scores in GLOBE; one for the "Former East" and another for the "Former West". I took the average of these two aggregate scores in order to match it with GEM's Germany-wide score.

– South Africa had two separate scores in GLOBE; one for the "Black Sample" and another for the "White Sample". I took the average of these two aggregate scores in order to match it with GEM's one South African score.

– Similarly, Switzerland had two separate scores in GLOBE; one for the "French-speaking" and another for the "German-speaking". I took the average of these two aggregate scores in order to match it with GEM's Switzerland-wide score.

– Canada's score in GLOBE represents the English-speaking culture only, where it is matched with Canada as a whole in GEM.

- England's score in GLOBE is matched with the United Kingdom's score in GEM.

Two types of Control Variables were used. The first are the dummies for each year (2004-2011), which were inserted in each model for pooling reasons and to control for the same-country, different-year observations. The second is a proxy for income. I initially used (GDP per capita at Purchasing Power Parity) but later replaced it with the (GDP per capita at PPP Growth; hereinafter "GDP/Capita Growth"). The adoption of GDP/Capita Growth as a control is based on two limitations/justifications. Firstly and most importantly, the use of (GDP per capita at PPP) as a control has presented a statistical challenge; where it has been found to have high collinearity with the independent variables. Secondly, there are strong arguments derived from the literature that support such adoption of "growth levels" instead of "static levels" of income. The "change" in income (or economic development) has been credited to have an impact on a main facet of entrepreneurship; i.e. self-employment rate. For example, a number of studies have found that economic "growth" has a negative impact on self-employment rates (Verheul et al., 2001; Schultz, 1990; Yamada,, 1996; Schaffner, 1993). Hence, GDP/Capita Growth is the best available and feasible control variable for the impact of economic development.

GDP/Capita Growth was calculated from the percentage increase in each year's (GDP per capita at PPP) score from the previous year. The source of the GDP data for all years is the International Monetary Fund (IMF) online database (www.imf.org). The limitation imposed by the sample size restricted the employment of further control variables.

The statistical method used in this study is a Pooled OLS (Ordinary Least Squares) regression analysis. The pooling was performed to control for the country observations that were dispersed across years. This has enabled the analysis to overcome the challenge of the unavailability of some country-scores for some years. As is customary, the year dummy variables and control variable were entered in the first block, followed by the independent variable in the second block. The primary software package used for performing the analyses and reporting the findings is IBM SPSS Version 19. Further analysis in STATA software was carried out to account for possible dependence in the residuals (command: cluster by); clustering by country. Results remained similar.

5. ANALYSIS AND RESULTS

5.1. The Main Effects:

The below table shows the correlation results and descriptives of all the variables:

Table 3

Descriptive Statistics and Correlations

		Mean	Std.	1	2	3	4	5	6	7	8
1	TEA	9.117	6.239								
2	Performance Orientation	4.052	.395	-.006							
3	Uncertainty Avoidance	4.167	.640	-.274***	.568***						
4	Institutional Collectivism	4.225	.479	-.189**	.495***	.51***					
5	In-Group Collectivism	4.969	.734	.422***	-.203***	-.651***	-.317***				
6	Assertiveness	4.133	.344	-.03	-.044	-.246***	-.578***	.114+			
7	Future Orientation	3.860	.485	-.285***	.669***	.79***	.607***	-.55***	-.112+		
8	Power Distance	5.151	.423	.232***	-.416***	-.62***	-.516***	.712***	.18**	-.676***	
9	GDP/Capita Growth	4.645	3.997	.224***	.068	.009	.118+	.256***	-.091	-.056	.091

N= 244, + p ≤ .10, * p ≤ .05, ** p ≤ .01, *** p ≤ .001

Some interesting correlations are worthy of highlighting. The dependent variable, TEA, is significantly correlated with: Uncertainty Avoidance (negatively), Institutional Collectivism (negatively), In-Group Collectivism (positively), Future Orientation (negatively), and Power Distance (positively). The significance scores of the above are all relatively very strong (all at 1% confidence levels). However, the correlation results between TEA and the other two variables (Performance Orientation and Assertiveness) are not significant. Overall, the significant correlations are all consistent with the study's initial expectations and hypotheses; except Future Orientation which has a contrary sign to the expected (negative instead of positive). The Control Variable (GDP/Capita Growth) is significantly correlated with TEA (positively), which is expected, as well as with In-Group Collectivism and, in a minimal degree, Institutional Collectivism (both positively). However, it is not significantly correlated with any other independent variable.

The results of the pooled regression analyses are reported below. Note that the variables (main and control) of each hypothesis were regressed separately:

Table 4

Cultural Determinants of Entrepreneurship
Dependent Variable: TEA

	Model 1	Model 2
Hypothesis 1:		
GDP/Capita Growth	.515 ***	.520 ***
Performance Orientation		-.036
Change in R2 from Model 1		.001
R2 (unadjusted)	.158	.159
R2 (adjusted)	.129	.127
F	5.517 ***	4.93 ***
Hypothesis 2:		
GDP/Capita Growth	.515 ***	.489 ***
Uncertainty Avoidance		-.239 ***
Change in R2 from Model 1		.055 ***
R2 (unadjusted)	.158	.213
R2 (adjusted)	.129	.183
F	5.517 ***	7.041 ***
Hypothesis 3:		
GDP/Capita Growth	.515 ***	.550 ***
Institutional Collectivism		-.231 ***
Change in R2 from Model 1		.052 ***
R2 (unadjusted)	.158	.210
R2 (adjusted)	.129	.180
F	5.517 ***	6.929 ***
Hypothesis 4:		
GDP/Capita Growth	.515 ***	.333 ***
In-Group Collectivism		.310 ***
Change in R2 from Model 1		.076 ***
R2 (unadjusted)	.158	.235
R2 (adjusted)	.129	.205
F	5.517 ***	7.967 ***

Hypothesis 5:

GDP/Capita Growth	.515 ***	.515 ***
Assertiveness		-.005
Change in R2 from Model 1		0
R2 (unadjusted)	.158	.158
R2 (adjusted)	.129	.126
F	5.517 ***	4.885 ***

Hypothesis 6:

GDP/Capita Growth	.515 ***	.468 ***
Future Orientation		.-.230 ***
Change in R2 from Model 1		.051 ***
R2 (unadjusted)	.158	.209
R2 (adjusted)	.129	.179
F	5.517 ***	6.878 ***

Hypothesis 7:

GDP/Capita Growth	.515 ***	.475 ***
Power Distance		.161 **
Change in R2 from Model 1		.025 **
R2 (unadjusted)	.158	.183
R2 (adjusted)	.129	.151
F	5.517 ***	5.814 ***

N= 244,   + p ≤ .10,   * p ≤ .05,   ** p ≤ .01,   *** p ≤ .001
Standardized beta coefficients are shown in the table.
Dummy variables for years (2004-2011) are inserted in each regression and results are available, but not reported in the above table due to space management reasons.

It is worth mentioning that this study, despite the limited number of observations and controls, is relatively unique in its ability to test (and find significant results) for the impact of national culture on entrepreneurship at the country level of analysis. As discussed earlier, studies in this specific domain are extremely rare or use mere correlations, if any.

In agreement with the correlation results, the table above shows that five of seven regressions are extremely significant, while two are not. In a general statement, the findings above confirm the role of national culture as a determinant for the aggregate levels of entrepreneurship across nations. This supports the notion, which was earlier expected, that each nation's culture does make a strong impact on its respective levels of entrepreneurial activity. Moreover, it could be observed that certain cultural practices have an impact, while there is no proof that other cultural practices do.

The regression results of H1 do not show a significant inferential relationship between the cultural dimension of Performance Orientation and TEA. Therefore, the predictability of this dimension is not established under this study's circumstances. The first hypothesis (H1) is then not fully supported. There is a discussion on a possible partial support in the following "Additional Analysis" section.

H2 regression results, on the other hand, show a great deal of significance. The R^2 is 0.213 at a below 1% significance level. The standardized coefficient (b) is 0.239 with an as anticipated negative sign. Hence, we could comfortably establish that Uncertainty Avoidance is a strong predictor of TEA. This leads us to conclude that the second hypothesis (H2) is supported.

H3 and H4 regressions test the two Collectivism hypotheses; Institutional and In-Group. As expected, both regressions show a very strong significance at a p-value of zero for both and R^2 of 0.21 and 0.235, respectively. The standardized beta coefficients are -0.231 for Institutional Collectivism and 0.31 for In-Group

Collectivism. The fact that both regressions are significant with an opposite coefficient sign (negative for Institutional and positive for In-Group) shows the strong yet reverse impact of each sub-dimension of collectivism. This may constitutes one of the most notable findings of this study and comfortably support hypotheses (H3 and H4).

H5 regression did not find a significant relationship between the cultural dimension of Assertiveness and TEA. Therefore, the predictability of this dimension in entrepreneurship levels is not established. And based on this, the fifth hypothesis (H5) is not fully supported. However, there are some insightful findings for this dimension which are discussed in the following "Additional Analysis" section.

H6 regression shows a strong significance at a p-value of zero and an R2 of 0.209. The standardized beta coefficient is found to be -0.23. This is one of the interesting findings as it is both significant yet the sign of the coefficient is contrary to the hypothesized relationship. Despite the fact that leads us to reject the relationship direction of hypothesis (H6), it provides us with valuable information to be analyzed. Hence, this suggests that the cultural dimension of Future Orientation has a negative impact on entrepreneurship levels.

H7 results illustrate a strong significance at the p-value of 0.008 and an R2 of 0.183, where the standardized coefficient (b) is at 0.161. The significance levels as well as the sign of the coefficient are in compliance with the study's expectations. Power Distance does display a positive impact on TEA. Therefore, the seventh and last hypothesis (H7) of this dissertation paper is clearly supported.

To summarize the above, four hypotheses (H2, H3, H4, and H7) are supported, two hypotheses (H1 and H5) are not supported, and one hypothesis (H6) is significant but with an opposite sign direction to the hypothesized.

5.2. Additional Analysis:

This section is an additional analysis to further understand the relationship between some dimensions of national culture and entrepreneurship. It is aimed to extend the investigation carried out in the previous section for the hypotheses that did not show significant results; namely, Performance Orientation and Assertiveness.

In doing so, the sample of 51 countries covered by this study were split into two sub-samples; High-Income and Low-Income. The method used to split the sample was based on each country's average (GDP per Capita at PPP) for all the studied years of 2004-2011. This resulted in two sub-samples: A High-Income sample of 25 countries, and a Low-Income sample of 24 countries.

Similar to the previous analysis, a Pooled OLS was also used for the two hypotheses (Performance Orientation and Assertiveness) in both sub-samples. Each hypothesis for each sub-sample was regressed separately; where the first block included the year dummy variables and the control variable, and the second block included the main effect variable. The main findings are reported in the following table:

Table 5

		High-Income Countries		Low-Income Countries	
		Coeff. & Sig.	*Coeff. Sign*	*Coeff. & Sig.*	*Coeff. Sign*
H1	Performance Orientation	.324 ***	+	Not Sig.	
H5	Assertiveness	.189 *	+	.194 +	-

+ p ≤ .10,   * p ≤ .05,   ** p ≤ .01,   *** p ≤ .001
Standardized beta coefficients are shown in the table.

Despite the fact that splitting the already-limited sample reduces its size; and hence, further restraining the regressions in finding informative results, there are relevant outcomes that should be highlighted. The first regression results – concerning the main effect of Performance Orientation (H1) shed more light on the nature of the relationship. Although it was not found to be significant in the main effect analysis, the results above suggest it is significant given a certain contextual setting. The hypothesis that argues for a positive impact of this cultural dimension on entrepreneurship is supported only within higher-income countries, yet within lower-income countries this argument is not necessarily true. A very high p-value (below 1% significance level) indicates its strong influence within this country income group. However, there is no proof of its impact in lower-income countries.

The Assertiveness dimension results (H5), on the other hand, are one of the more interesting. Recalling the earlier main effect analysis, results failed to find significance. However, the results of this additional analysis had two findings: 1) The hypothesis is supported in the higher-income countries sample (positive impact of Assertiveness on entrepreneurship), and 2) The contrary is found in the lower-income countries sample (negative impact of Assertiveness on entrepreneurship). Hence, it seems that this dimension has a totally contrasting attitude towards entrepreneurship based on the level of country income. It could be stated, with conservations, that this dimension fosters entrepreneurship when the income levels of the country are relatively high, but it does the opposite when they are relatively low.

This dissertation has also attempted to do a third analysis (not reported) in the aim to further analyze the impact of income on the relationship between culture and entrepreneurship. This analysis ran regression analyses with (GDP per Capita at PPP) as a moderator; intersecting it with each cultural dimension separately. The findings proved to be well in-line with the findings of the main effect analysis and the data-splitting analysis. Regardless of its strong supporting findings, it was dismissed and not reported due to the same earlier-mentioned statistical barrier; i.e. high collinearity with the independent variables.

6. DISCUSSION AND CONCLUSIONS

The theoretical logic and empirical results of this study indicate that establishing a bridge between cultural studies and entrepreneurship literature helps researchers to better understand the "why" and "how" questions behind the prosperity of entrepreneurship - as a vital component of economical revitalization - in some nations compared to others. The need for understanding these questions has never been more vital and pressing than today. This is due to the obvious turbulent and changing economical landscape and crises that have touched the everyday life of millions around the world (some positively, and many negatively). Hence, a fresh look into the determinants and factors influencing the "engine of economies", i.e. entrepreneurship, is extremely relevant to researchers, policy makers, and entrepreneurial individuals alike.

This dissertation has responded to the researchers' call to explore whether culture makes a difference at the country level of analysis (e.g. McGrath, MacMillan, Yang, & Tsai, 1992), where the scarcity of studies on the culture's impact constitutes a gap in the entrepreneurship literature (Berger, 1991; Davidsson, 1995; Begley & Tan, 2001). In doing so, this dissertation has established a theoretical justification and empirical assessment of the national culture's influence on the systematic variation of national entrepreneurship levels relative to other nations. It has uncovered the impact of a number of cultural dimensions on the level of entrepreneurship (in the nation level of analysis); identifying the ones that are associated with higher entrepreneurial activity (functional/fostering) and the ones that are associated with lower activity (dysfunctional/inhabiting). This dissertation has also attempted to assess many of the popular measures of the entrepreneurship and national culture constructs; putting forward the most valid and relevant ones and criticizing some of the handicapped ones. It is also worth noting that this study has allowed the combination and utilization of two leading global projects, GEM and GLOBE, in a relevant and constructive approach to the two respective fields of literature.

The findings of the research have supported the notion that culture, at the country level of analysis, makes a strong difference in entrepreneurship levels. This could be observed in the extremely significant regression results of most of the studied cultural dimensions. This finding should help in highlighting the role played by national culture to interested parties; rather than solely focusing on the traditional factors influencing entrepreneurship such as financing and micro-financing, legal frameworks, licensing procedures, VCs, and export insurances. Culture, as established here, functions as a hidden driving force behind the efficiency and effectiveness of any national incentive campaigns geared toward the development of new ventures and SME sectors. National culture could act as a limiting or opportunity-making reality to each nation. A careful analysis and understanding of the national culture's composition is vital when planning as well as executing any initiatives or measures aimed toward this goal.

More specifically, this dissertation paper has found certain cultural dimensions to be fostering or inhabiting to the growth of entrepreneurship levels. The cultural dimension of Uncertainty Avoidance, for instance, has proved to entail a negative impact on the tendency of the population to engage in entrepreneurial activities. Austria and Denmark are two good examples for this; where their Uncertainty Avoidance levels rank amongst the highest in the world (5.16 and 5.22; respectively). This reality has been a major factor in their poor entrepreneurship levels; where they project some of the lowest TEA levels at an average of 3.86 and 4.22; respectively. The fear of the unknown and preference of having rules, order, and a stable career paths, do contradict the essence of entrepreneurship; where the assumption of insecurity, tolerance of ambiguity, and probability of failure are essential parts of it. It should be noted, however, that this concept should not be confused with "risk avoidance" in, for example, business decisions. Risk avoidance and uncertainty avoidance are two different concepts; where "uncertainty is to risk as anxiety to fear" (Hofstede, 2001). If uncertainty becomes quantified – as in the case of risk, it ceases to be anxious to its beholder. Uncertainty avoidance aims to escape from ambiguity, not risk. Some cultures are relatively comfortable with the ambiguity poised by venturing in a confident bet towards its fruits of higher profits, autonomy, and/or the mere chance of trying new things. It is important to note that such cultural traits are built (or not) within the common sense of the majority of people through a long historical heritage; manifested in institutions, school systems, family upbringing, tales, heroes, idols, religions, etc. and not easily altered or changed (on the aggregate level, not the individual case). Hence, we could verify that the relatively high uncertainty avoidance, as a cultural characteristic, inhibits the supply of entrepreneurship and entrepreneurs in a given nation. Vice versa, the opposite of this dimension – comfort with uncertainty and ambiguity – fosters it.

On the other hand, the cultural dimension and practice of Power Distance has been proved to have a positive influence on levels of entrepreneurship, in opposite to what some researchers have claimed or expected. For example, Thailand, Nigeria, and Ecuador possess some of the highest scores in this cultural dimension; which have consequentially supported their high entrepreneurship levels (on average, more than 20% of their populations are engaged in entrepreneurial activities). Having a culture that expects and agrees that power should be unequally shared (or concentrated) is favorable to entrepreneurship. This unequal sharing of power and authority is not necessarily inhumane; as it may have stemmed from a perceived expertise, knowledge, or personality of the higher power holder by the beholder. Nations with relatively lower power distance, such as the Netherlands, would assume that opportunities should be equally accessed and privileges equally shared and, hence, power. The main essence of such value system is the mere detest of power, where it is believed to be a corrupting factor. However, there are also less humane justifications of having a high power distance culture that are not based on perceived expertise of else. For example, nations that are heavily structured in a class system of any sort do tend to bring along undeserved privileges to the "more powerful" – such as access to information, opportunities, financing, networks, etc. – which, in turn, provide them with unfairly-possessed, enabling-tools for a successful new venture.

However, this cultural dimension received a great attention but contradictive findings from the field's scholars. This dissertation paper tried to solve this flux of paradoxical propositions. One camp of scholars advocated the argument of the need of a lower power distance cultures for entrepreneurship to flourish (e.g. Wu, 2007; Mueller et al., 2002; Mitchell et al., 2000; Shane, 1992;1993), while the other camp argued the opposite (McGrath, MacMillan, & Scheinberg, 1992; Wildeman et al., 1999; Verheul et al., 2002). This dissertation has supported the second camp's notion, and has empirically proved it. The reasons behind this study's support for this notion are based on a number of reasons: the escalation of the need for "catching up" of the less powerful (Brenner, 1987) in high power distance cultures; manifested in a human need to be their own bosses at an unequal environment. This is also in line with a popular argument in the literature; that entrepreneurs cannot accept authority (Hagen, 1962). This idea counters the first camp's expectation of low entrepreneurship when there inequality and limited access to resources. Instead of this reality being a constant constraint (see above argument – e.g. Mitchell et al., 2000), it actually triggers a strong human need to overcome it; i.e. catch up. Moreover, the feeling of dissatisfaction with the status quo in the work environment constitutes a major factor influencing the individual decision to venture out (Collins et al., 1964; Shapero, 1975). Researchers have argued that a culture of high inequality, suppressive nature, and wide salary differences (high power distance) will create particular incentives for starting a new business and a source of entrepreneurship (Verheul et al., 2002; MacGrath, MacMillan, & Scheinberg, 1992; Wildeman et al., 1999). This is in addition to the ventures created by the more powerful segment of the population due to their "special" access and resources. Hence, a culture that is described to have high inequality in power distribution, wide salary differences and suppressive nature has found to be having higher level of entrepreneurial activity. Needless to say, this should not be perceived as a prescribed road map for fostering entrepreneurship in a nation, rather as a realistic view of the important dynamics played by national culture in this regard.

One of the most insightful and novel relationships and findings of this dissertation could be the ones regarding Collectivism. Despite it being one of the most discussed cultural dimensions in the entrepreneurship literature, it has been widely misread. A long-lasting tradition among scholars fiercely associated individualism with entrepreneurship (e.g. Mitchell et al., 2000; McGrath, MacMillan, & Scheinberg, 1992); leading some authoritative figures to declare that an individualistic society is entrepreneurial by definition (McClelland, 1961). However, empirical tests that have been built on this argument have either found no proof (Mueller et al., 2002), opposite findings (Wu, 2007; Baum et al., 1993), or mixed findings (Bhawuk & Udas, 1996). This dissertation, however, tried to have a more in-depth analysis of this seemingly-confusing construct since an early stage of this paper's development. It has found that the common adoption of this cultural dimension at face-value is misleading. This is due to the fact that there are two levels to it – e.g. horizontal and vertical – which have been discussed earlier. The two levels carry different attributes of collectivism that should be treated independently; as they capture two theoretically different aspects and, consequentially, have two totally distinct implications on entrepreneurship – one negative/hindering and the other positive/encouraging. Institutional Collectivism, which encourages uniformity across its members, collective action, and the prioritizes the societal gains over individual ones, has been argued and proven to be disadvantageous to entrepreneurship. Reflected in societal practices such as the "loss of face" in some Asian cultures, this sub-dimension of collectivism plays against the individual and competitive act of entrepreneurship. This study confirmed that Institutional Collectivism has a negative impact on entrepreneurship levels.

On the other hand, the more "vertical" In-Group Collectivism carries different attributes. It reflects the degree of a culture's emphasis on individual and immediate-family gains, loyalty, inter-reliance, and pride. It also reflects the prioritization of personal gains over the wide-society's gains. As a personal practice that may requires the support of immediate-family and immediate-friends, entrepreneurship should be fully aligned with this sub-dimension of collectivism. The findings do confirm this study's expectation; where In-Group Collectivism has a positive impact on entrepreneurship levels at the country level of analysis.

Additional notable findings should also be highlighted. Future Orientation, for instance, showed a contrary sign direction to the expected. This study earlier expected, in line with the general trend in the literature (e.g. Busenitz & Lau, 1997; Takyi-Asiedu, 1993), that entrepreneurship stems from a cultural practice that acknowledges future/time as a commodity, engages in calculated risk ventures, delays gratification, and adopts planning as a tool to minimize future challenges or hurdles. However, the findings suggest the opposite. It seems to support the idea that higher levels of entrepreneurship stems from cultures that are more spontaneous, pay less emphasis on planning and strategies, and generally live "in the moment". This is indeed an interesting, yet unexpected, finding that should be further explored. Cultures that are more planning-oriented may have perceived entrepreneurship to be too risky, unfeasible, or too ambiguous. Hence, it could be concluded that a high Future Orientation profile in a culture negatively impacts its entrepreneurship levels.

The cultural dimension of Performance Orientation has also found a marginal support in certain contexts. This study found that the expected positive impact of this dimension on entrepreneurship could only be true in higher-than-average-income countries. It seems to be a specific dimension that comes to play only when income is higher than average. It seizes to show a significant impact in lower income countries. One could justify this to the priorities of needs in a given culture. When the disposable income is available and/or rising, the need for out-performing peers, efficiency, and innovation may lead people to venture out and put this into practice. However, when the priority is directed towards a stable income and career, this performance-attribute may manifest itself in performing/excelling at government job or a reliable corporate job. There, it allows for a restricted projection of performance-related attributes while still brings food to the table.

The findings of the Assertiveness dimension are also one of the interesting ones. The results display a 2-way contrasting influences of this dimension on entrepreneurship. It seems that the implications of having a highly assertive culture are polarized. In the context of higher-than-average-income countries, this dimension seems to have a positive impact on entrepreneurship. However, in lower income countries, this impact becomes negative. So, it could be said, with caution, that the assertive culture, which entails toughness, aggressiveness, dominance, and masculine attributes encourages entrepreneurship only if coupled with a higher income level in that country. The reverse concept of this dimension – passiveness - seems to be the entrepreneurship-promoting factor in lower-income countries. This, indeed, constitutes a promising area for further investigation as it brings up a new debate to this little-covered dimension in the literature.

In summary, this dissertation has attempted to bridge a literature gap (e.g. Berger, 1991; Davidsson, 1995; Begley & Tan, 2001) in the understanding of the national culture's role in entrepreneurship; where it has carried vitally-relevant implications on both the academic and practitioner worlds. It has added to the academic fields of entrepreneurship, sociology, and international business by: 1) Providing evidence for the strong impact of culture on entrepreneurship at the country level of analysis through a rare study that covered 51 countries across various and distinct cultural settings. 2) Assessing the cultural dimensions that foster or inhibit the aggregate entrepreneurship levels; shedding light on the previously-dark and vague side that ignited/obstructed such activity in the first place. 3) Solved a number of contradicting/ opposing findings with due justification and subsequent empirical testing. 4) Established and tested new associations with cultural dimensions – and sub-dimensions - that have never been directly studied in this regard with novel theorization and findings. 5) Criticized with due justifications some of the popular, yet handicapped, measures of entrepreneurship and national culture; in an effort to elect the more accurate and valid ones. And 6) Carried a study that allowed the useful combination and utilization of two of the largest research projects in the field; GLOBE and GEM.

This dissertation has also significant implications on the practitioner world; that should interest both policy makers and entrepreneurs (including potential entrepreneurs). Most governments and public service leaders acknowledge the fruitful consequences of promoting entrepreneurship on their respective economies and even social/political stability; as it constitutes a major source of new jobs and a central cornerstone to the growth of income and GDP. Such argument cannot be more important than today; where social stability has been shaken in most of the developed and developing worlds. And where most public frustrations, strikes, and even revolutions have mainly stemmed from the shrinking of public and personal income; and the diminishing pool of new jobs. Historically, governments have employed numerous initiatives and programs to incentivize SME (Small and Medium Enterprises) development and entrepreneurship. However, the positive impact of such endeavors has been largely questioned (e.g. Mueller et al., 2002), since most overlook their fitness to local contexts (Dubini, 1988; Davidsson et al., 1994). This dissertation has provided aiding tools to determine such fitness and to develop more relevant initiatives and programs to each distinctive culture. In contrast to merely copying other nation's successful programs (which may or may not be suitable), the findings of this study provide an assessment of the cultural dimensions that have a direct positive/negative impact on entrepreneurship. Policy makers should set their prioritizations towards that "fostering" cultural dimensions; developing programs that support and embrace them. And vice versa with the "inhibiting" cultural dimensions. Their efforts should be focused on initiatives that alleviate/discourage the negative impact of the "inhibiting" cultural dimensions and support/embrace the positive impact of the "fostering" dimensions; through education, training programs, and awareness campaigns. Moreover, initiatives should also be focused on ones that are not drastically different and distant from the existing cultural context. Despite the relatively-longer process in adopting such methods, curing the root of the problem is the more sustainable and efficient solution. This will also result in a more efficient allocation of national resources and efforts – towards the areas that matter the most. Professional practitioners; entrepreneurs and potential entrepreneurs, could also be able to gain a better comprehension of particular factors or threats that are critical to the existence of their ventures. The findings of this study should allow them to recognize essential dynamics that come into action and are crucial to the introduction and sustainability of their entrepreneurial ventures; for example, in aspects of finding the needed entrepreneurial human resources, cultural acceptability of such start-ups, and the general attitudes of the collective community. It could also aid their assessment and set their expectations when aiming to evaluate a location for their new ventures.

Finally, I would like to conclude this section with some words that caught my attention (for good or bad) during the years of researching this topic:

- *"If you see in any given situation only what everybody else can see, you can be said to be so much representative of your culture than you are a victim of it".* S. I. Hayakawa

- *"Historians will have to face the fact that natural selection determined the evolution of cultures in the same manner as it did that of species".* Konrad Lorenz

7. LIMITATIONS AND FUTURE RESEARCH

As it is the case in any study, there are a number of limitations. There has been some criticism in the validity of using the national or geographical boundaries as units of analysis (Lenartowicz & Roth, 1999). Some argue that such unit of analysis may be too broad and may not best capture the sub-cultures within a country (Chrisman, Chua, & Steier, 2002); which some found to be existing and distinguishable in a country like Brazil (Lenartowicz & Roth, 2001). They suggest that studies of culture should focus more on uncovering its many nuances and dimensions. However, an opposing group of researchers consent that nations (or countries) provide us with probably the only kinds of units available for comparing cultures (e.g. Hofstede, 2001). As stated earlier in this dissertation, Kluckhohn & Strodtbeck (1961) argue that "a national culture is a fairly consistent set of value orientations developed in response to the fact that there are a limited number of common societal problems with a limited number of known responses". Nations are capable of creating tenuous ties that form shared perceptions even though members of this group – or nation, in this case – might not know one another (e.g. attitudes towards business or a sports team that are very specific to a region). Hofstede (2001) also argue that national borders are the most suitable for cultural comparisons because mechanisms promoting cultural similarities such as the educational and law systems, as well as the language, are usually shared at the national level. Additionally, the purpose of any study should be the one dictating the most suitable unit of analysis. A study of sub-cultures, as argued above, should serve a purpose of analyzing the underlying dynamics at play within a given country or multiple-cultures environment, which is not the case in this dissertation. Otherwise, this will lead us to break units of analysis endlessly while losing the opportunity to make sense of the information. For instance, even sub-cultures have their own sub-cultures (e.g. men/women, old/young, education level, religion, etc.). Since, the purpose of this dissertation is to uncover the role of the whole-country's culture in supplying entrepreneurs and entities across regions and sub-cultures, our unit of analysis of nations is the most practical for this goal.

The GLOBE sample is limited to middle managers across various organizations. Hence, some would argue that we be cautious in generalizing the findings to the whole culture. However, strong correlations of GLOBE data with unobtrusive measures that reflect the broader society were found. This, in turn, means that GLOBE could be assumed to reflect the broader culture in which middle managers are embedded rather than the cultures of the middle managers only (for more details, see House et al., 2004 – pg. 20).

The investigation of the impact of other cultural dimensions – in addition to the ones studied here - on entrepreneurship is also worth exploring. The remaining dimensions of GLOBE (Humane Orientation and Gender Egalitarianism – see definitions in TABLE 1) have not been studied here due to the lack of theoretically appealing and relevant justifications. However, they may well have a direct or indirect influence on this relationship. Other new and independent cultural dimensions could also be explored.

Despite the fact that it is very rare and very expensive to obtain matched and comparable cross-country data at the aggregate level, it would be much more enlightening to have data from more countries than the ones in this dissertation paper. Having an even larger sample that include more countries would have given us an opportunity to more adequately test our hypotheses. It is worth mentioning that studies of this scale and coverage are very rare in most fields of management research.

Future research could also build on the findings of this dissertation paper by extending the relationship between national culture and aggregate levels of entrepreneurship. The extension could examine the impact of this relationship not only on the levels of entrepreneurship but also on the type of the entrepreneurial ventures created. The size, economical motivation (necessity vs. opportunity), and structure (single establishment, partnership, etc.) are all possible investigative areas of the type of such entrepreneurial activity. Another commendable area of research is the examination of the role played by the family in moderating or adjusting the impact of national culture. The study of other roles played by the institutional entities present in a given nation is also a plausible future extension; such as governments, schools, professional associations, cartels, etc.

8. BIBLIOGRAPHY

Acs, Z. J. (1992). Small business economics: A global perspective. *Challenge*, 35(6): 38-44.

Acs, Z. J. (2006). How is entrepreneurship good for economic growth? *Innovations*, 97–106.

Adler, N. J., Doktor, R., and Redding, S. G. (1986). From the Atlantic to the Pacific century: Cross-cultural management reviewed. *Journal of Management*, 12(2), 295-318.

Aldrich, H. E., and Cliff, J. E. (2003). The pervasive effects of family on entrepreneurship: Toward a family embeddedness perspective. *Journal of Business Venturing*, 18(5), 573–596.

Aldrich, H., and Zimmer, C. (1986). Entrepreneurship Through Social Networks. In D. L. Sexton and R. W. Smilor (eds.), *The Art and Science of Entrepreneurship,* pp. 2-23. Cambridge, MA: Ballinger Publishing.

Amit, R., Glosten, L., and Muller, E. (1993). Challenges to theory development in entrepreneurship research. *Journal of Management Studies*, 30(5):815–834.

Anderson, A. R. and Miller, C. J. (2003). Class matters: human and social capital in the entrepreneurial process. *Journal of Socio-Economics*, 32, 17–36.

Anderson, A. R. and Smith, R. (2007). The moral space in entrepreneurship: an exploration of ethical imperatives and the moral legitimacy of being enterprising. *Entrepreneurship and Regional Development*, 19, 479–497.

Ansoff, H. I. (1988). *The New Corporate Strategy*. New York: John Wiley.

Aronson, R. L. (1991). *Self-employment: A labor market perspective*. Ithaca, NY: ILR Press.

Audretsch, D. M. and Thurik, A. R. (2000). Capitalism and democracy in the 21st century; from the managed to the entrepreneurial economy. *Journal of Evolutionary Economics*, 10, 17–34.

Baker, T., Gedajlovic, E., and Lubatkin, M. (2005). A framework for comparing entrepreneurial processes across nations. *Journal of International Business Studies*, 36: 492-504.

Bartunek, J. M. (1984). Changing interpretive scheme and organizational restructuring: The example of a religious order. *Administrative Science Quarterly*, 29(3), 355-372.

Baughn, C. C., Chua, B. L., and Neupert, K. E. (2006). The normative context for women's participation in entrepreneurship: A multicountry study. *Entrepreneurship Theory and Practice*, 30(5), 687-708.

Baum, J. R., Olian, J. D., Erez, M., Schnell, E. R., Smith, K. G., Sims, H. P., Scully, J. S., and Smith, K. A. (1993). Nationality and work role interactions: a cultural contrast of Israeli and U.S. entrepreneurs' versus managers' needs. *Journal of Business Venturing*, 8 (6), 499-512.

Becker, G. A. (1965). Theory of the allocation of time. *The Economic Journal*, 75, 493-517.

Begley, T. M. and Boyd, D. P. (1987). Psychological characteristics associated with performance in entrepreneurial firms and smaller businesses. *Journal of Business Venturing*, 2:79–93.

Begley, T. M. and Tan, W. (2001). The socio-cultural environment for entrepreneurship: A comparison between East Asian and Anglo-Saxon countries. *Journal of International Business Studies*, 32(3), 537–553.

Berger, B. (1991). *The Culture of Entrepreneurship*. San Francisco: Institute for Contemporary Studies.

Bernardo, A., and Welch, I. (2001). On the evolution of overconfidence of entrepreneurs. *Journal of Economics and Management Strategy*, 10: 301-330.

Bhawuk, D. P. S., & Udas, A. (1996). *Entrepreneurship and collectivism: A study of Nepalese entrepreneurs*. In J. Pandey, D. Sinha, & D. P. S.

Bhawuk (eds.), *Asian Contributions to Cross Cultural Psychology*, (pp. 307-317). New Delhi: Sage.

Bird, B. (1989). *Entrepreneurial Behavior*. Glenville, IL: Scott Foresman.

Birley, S. (1985). The role of networks in the entrepreneurial process. *Journal of Business Venturing*, I(1): 107-I 17.

Blanchflower, D. G. (2000). Self-employment in OECD countries. *Labour Economics*, 7, 471–505.

Blanchflower, D. G. and Oswald, A. J. (1998). What makes a entrepreneur. *Journal of Labor Economics*, 16: 26-60.

Bluedorn, A. C. (2000). *Time and Organizational Culture*. In N. M. Ashkanasy, Celeste. P. M. Wilderom, and Mark. F. Peterson (eds.), *Handbook of Organizational Culture and Climate*, pp. 117-128. Thousand Oaks, CA: Sage Publications.

Bond, M. H. and Pang, M. K. (1989). *Trusting to the Tao: Chinese values and the re-centering of psychology*. Paper presented at the Conference on Moral Values and Moral Reasoning in Chinese Societies, Taipei, Taiwan.

Brenner, O. C., Tomkiewicz, J., and Schein, V. E. (1989). The relationship between sex role stereotypes and requisite management characteristics revisited. *Academy of Management Journal*, 32, 662-669.

Brenner, R. (1987). National policy and entrepreneurship: The statesman's dilemma. *Journal of Business Venturing*, 2(2):95-101.

Brockhaus, R. H. (1982). *The psychology of the entrepreneur.* In Kent, C. A., Sexton, D. L., and Vesper, K. H. (eds.), *Encyclopedia of Entrepreneurship.* New York: Prentice-Hall, Inc.

Brockhaus, R. H. (1987). Entrepreneurial folklore. *Journal of Small Business Management*, Vol. 25, July, No. 3, 1-6.

Brockhaus, R. H. Sr. and Horwitz, P. S. (1986). *The Psychology of Entrepreneurship.* In: D. L. Sexton and R. W. Smilor (eds.), *The Art and Science of Entrepreneurship*, Cambridge, MA: Ballinger/ Englewood Cliffs, NJ: Prentice-Hall.

Brüderal, J. and Preisendörfer, P. (1998). Network support and the success of newly founded businesses. *Small Business Economics*, 10: 213-225.

Bruton, G. D., Ahlstrom, D., and Li, H. L. (2010). Institutional theory and entrepreneurship: Where are we now and where do we need to move in the future?. *Entrepreneurship Theory and Practice*, 34:3, 421-440.

Busenitz, L. W. and Lau, C. M. (1997). A cross-cultural cognitive model of new venture creation. *Entrepreneurship Theory and Practice*, 20(4), 25–39.

Busenitz, L. W., Gomez, C, & Spencer, J. W. (2000). Country institutional profiles: Unlocking entrepreneurial phenomena. *Academy of Management Journal*, 43, 994-1003.

Carland, J. W., Hoy, F., Boulton, W. R., and Carland, J. A. (1984). Differentiating entrepreneurs from small business owners: a conceptualization. *Academy of Management Review*, 9, 354–359.

Casson, M. (1990). *Enterprise and Competitiveness*. New York: Oxford University Press.

Chiles, T. H., Bluedorn, A. C., and Gupta, V. K. (2007). Beyond creative destruction and entrepreneurial discovery: A radical Austrian approach to entrepreneurship. *Organization Studies*, 28(4): 467-493.

Chrisman, J. J., Chua, J. H., and Steier, L. P. (2002). The influence of national culture and family involvement on entrepreneurial perceptions and performance at the state level. *Entrepreneurship: Theory and Practice*, 26(4), 113-129.

Cochran, T. C. (1949). Role and Sanction in American Entrepreneurial History. In *Change and the Entrepreneur: Postulates and Patterns for Entrepreneurial History*: Harvard Research Center in Entrepreneurial History.

Collins, O. F., Moore, D. G., and Unwalla, D. B. (1964). *The Enterprising Man*. East Lansing, MI: Michigan State University Business Studies.

Collins, R. (2004). *Interaction Ritual Chains*. Princeton, NJ: Princeton University Press.

Cooper, A., Woo C., and Dunkelberg, W. (1988). Entrepreneurs' perceived chances for success. *Journal of Business Venturing*, 3: 97-108.

Crawford, M. (1995). *Talking Difference: On Gender and Language*. London: Sage.

Cyret, R. M. and March, J. G. (1963). *A Behavioral Theory of the Firm*. Englewood Cliffs, NJ: Prentice Hall.

Daft, R. L., & Weick, K. E. (1984). Toward a model of organizations as interpretation systems. *Academy of Management Review*, 9(2), 284-295.

Davidsson, P. (1995). Culture, structure and regional levels of entrepreneurship. *Entrepreneurship and Regional Development*, 7, 41-62.

Davidsson, P. and Wiklund, J. (1997). Values, beliefs and regional variations in new firm formation rates. *Journal of Economic Psychology*, 18, 179-199.

Davidsson, P. and Wiklund, J. (2001). Levels of analysis in entrepreneurship research: current research practice and suggestions for the future. *Entrepreneurship Theory & Practice*, 25 (3), 81–99.

Davidsson, P., Lindmark, L., and Olofsson, C. (1994). New firm formation and regional development in Sweden. *Regional Studies*, Vol. 28, pp. 395-410.

Davis J. A., Pitts E. L., and Cormier, K. (2000). Challenges facing family companies in the Gulf Region. *Family Business Review*, 13(3), 217-237.

DiMaggio, P. J. and Powell, W. W. (1983). The iron cage revisited: Institutional isomorphism and collective rationality in organizational fields. *American Sociological Review*, 48: 147-160.

DiMaggio, P. J. and Powell, W. W. (1991). *Introduction*. In W. W. Powell and P. J. DiMaggio (eds.), *The New Institutionalism in Organizational Analysis* (pp. 1–38). Chicago: University of Chicago Press.

Doney, P. M., Cannon, J. P., and Mullen, M. R. (1988). Understanding the influence of national culture on the development of trust. *Academy of Management Review*, 23: 601-620.

Dubini, P. (1988). Motivational and environmental influences on business start ups: Some hints for public policy. Journal of Business Venturing, 4, 11-26.

Earley, P. C. (1997). *Face, Harmony and Social Structure: An Analysis of Organizational Behavior across Cultures*. New York: Oxford University Press.

Elam, A. and Terjesen, S. (2007) *Institutional Logics: Gender and Business Creation Across GEM Countries*. In: Frontiers of Entrepreneurship Research 2007.

El-Harbi, S. and Anderson, A. R. (2010). Institutions and the shaping of different forms of entrepreneurship. *The Journal of Socio-Economics*, XXX

Engelen, A., Heinemann, F., and Brettel, M. (2009). Cross-cultural entrepreneurship research: Current status and framework for future studies. *Journal of International Entrepreneurship*, 7:3, 163-189.

Etzioni, A. (1987). *The European Observatory for SMEs: Fourth Annual Report*. Zoetermeer: EIM Business and Policy Research.

Fagenson, E. A. (1990). Perceived masculine and feminine attributes examined as a function of individual's sex and level in the organizational power hierarchy: A test of four theoretical perspectives. *Journal of Applied Psychology*, 75, 204-211.

Fagenson, E. A. (1993). Personal value systems of men and women entrepreneurs versus managers. *Journal of Business Venturing*, 8, 409-430.

French, J. R. P. and Raven, B. (1959). *The bases of social power.* In D. Cartwright and A. Zander (eds.), *Group Dynamics* (3rd ed., pp. 259-269). New York: Harper & Row.

Gartner, W. B. (1985). A conceptual framework for describing the phenomenon of new venture creation. *Academy of Management Review*, 10(4), 696-706.

George, G. and Zahra, S. A. (2002) Culture and its consequences for entrepreneurship. *Entrepreneurship Theory and Practice*, 26(4): 5–7.

Gomez-Mejia, L. R., Haynes, K., Jacobson, K., Nuñez-Nickel, M., and Moyano, J. (2007). Socioemotional wealth and business risks in family-controlled firms: Evidence from Spanish olive oil mills. *Administrative Science Quarterly*, 52(1): 106–137.

Gompers, P. A., Lerner, J., and Scharfstein, D. (2005). Entrepreneurial spawning: Public corporations and the genesis of new ventures, 1986 to 1999. *Journal of Finance*, 60(2), 577–614.

Granovetter, M. (1985). Economic action and social structure: The problem of embeddedness. *American Journal of Sociology*, 91, 481-510.

Gupta, V. K. and Fernandez, C. (2009). Cross-cultural similarities and differences in characteristics attributed to entrepreneurs: A three nation study. *Journal of Leadership and Organizational Studies*, 15(3), 304-318.

Gupta, V., Levenburg, N., Moore, L. L., Motwani, J., and Schwarz, T. V. (2008). Exploring the construct of family business in the emerging markets. *The International Journal of Business and Emerging Markets*, 1(2); 189-208.

Habbershon, T. G. and Pistrui, J. (2002). Enterprising families domain: Family-influenced ownership groups in pursuit of transgenerational wealth. *Family Business Review*, 15(3): 223-237.

Hagen, E. E. (1962). *On the Theory of Social Change: How Economic Growth Begins*. Homewood, IL: Dorsey Press.

Hall, E. T. (1973). *The Silent Language*. Garden City NJ: Anchor Books.

Hayton, J. C., George, G., and Zahra, S. A. (2002). National culture and entrepreneurship: A review of behavioral research. *Entrepreneurship Theory and Practice*, 26(4), 33–52.

Hofstede, G. (1980). *Culture's Consequences: International Differences in Work-Related Values.* Sage Publications, Newbury Pk, CA.

Hofstede, G. (1983a). *Dimensions of national cultures in fifty countries and three regions.* In J. B. Deregowski, S. Dziurawiec, & R. C, Annis (eds). Expiscations in Cross-Cultural Psychology, Swets & Zeitlinger, Lisse, Netherlands, 1983, p. 335-355.

Hofstede, G. (1983b). National cultures in four dimensions. *International Studies of Management and Organization*, 13, 46-74.

Hofstede, G. (1983c). The cultural relativity of organizational practices and theories. *Journal of International Business Studies*, 14, 75-89.

Hofstede, G. (1983d). National cultures revisited. *Behavior Science Research*, 18, 285-305.

Hofstede, G. (1984). The cultural relativity of the quality of life concept. *The Academy of Management Review*, 9:3, 389-398.

Hofstede, G. (2001). *Culture's Consequences,* (2nd ed.) Thousand Oaks, CA: Sage.

Hofstede, G. (1991). *Cultures and Organizations: Software of the Mind.* London: McGraw Hill.

Hofstede, G. and Bond, M. H. (1988). The Confucius connection: From cultural roots to economic growth. *Organizational Dynamics*, 16(4), p. 4-21.

Hofstede, G., Neuijen, B., Ohayv, D. D., and Sanders, G. (1990). Measuring organizational cultures: A qualitative and quantitative study across twenty cases. *Administrative Science Quarterly, 35,* 286-316.

House, R. J., Hanges, P. J., Javidan, M., Dorfman, P., and Gupta, V. (2004). *Culture, Leadership, and Organizations: The GLOBE Study of 62 Societies*, Thousand Oaks, CA: Sage.

House, R. J., Javidan, M., and Dorfman, P. (2001). The Globe Project. *Applied Psychology: An International Review*, 50:4, 489-505.

Hundley, G. (2001). Why and when are the self-employed more satisfied with their work?. *Industrial Relations*, 40: 293-317.

Ireland, R. D., Hitt, M. A., and Sirmon, D. G. (2003). A model of strategic entrepreneurship: The construct and its dimensions. *Journal of Management*, Vol. 29 pp.963 - 989.

Jepperson, R. (1991). *Institutions, institutional effects, and institutionalism*. In W. W. Powell and P. J. DiMaggio (eds.), *The new Institutionalism in Organizational Analysis* (pp. 143–163). Chicago: University of Chicago Press.

Keough, K. A., Zimbardo, P. G., and Boyd, J. N. (1999). Who's smoking, drinking, and using drugs? Time perspective as a predictor of substance use', *Basic and Applied Social Psychology*, 21(2): 149–64.

Kluckhohn, F. and Strodtbeck, F. L. (1961). *Variations in Value Orientations*, Evanston, IL: Row Peterson.

Knight, G. A. (1997). Cross-cultural reliability and validity of a scale to measure firm entrepreneurial orientation. *Journal of Business Venturing*, 12: 213-225.

Kroeber, A. L. and Parsons, T. (1958). The concepts of culture and of social system. *American Sociological Review*, 23, 582-583.

Kuratko, D. F. (2007). Entrepreneurial leadership in the 21st century. *Journal of Leadership and Organizational Studies,* 13(4).

Lange, A. J. and Jabuwkoski, P. (1976). Key issues in the development of aggression and violence from childhood to early adulthood. *Annual Review of Psychology*, 48, 371-410.

Lenartowicz, T., and Roth, K. (1999). A framework for culture assessment. *Journal of International Business Studies, 30(4),* 761-798.

Lenartowicz, T., and Roth, K. (2001). Does subculture within a country matter: A cross-cultural study of motivational domains and business performance in Brazil. *Journal of International Business Studies, 32(2),* 305-325.

Lewin, K. (1942). *Time Perspective and Morale.* In G. Watson (ed.) *Civilian Morale.* Boston, MA: Houghton, Mifflin.

Licht, A. N. and Siegel, J. I. (2005). *The Social Dimensions of Entrepreneurship.* In Casson, M., Yeung, B. (eds.), *Oxford Handbook of Entrepreneurship,* Oxford University Press, Oxford (2006).

Lockett, M. (1987). China's special economic zones: The cultural and managerial challenges. *Journal of General Management,* 12(3), 21-31.

Louis, M. R. (1980). Surprise and sense making: What newcomers experience in entering unfamiliar organizational settings. *Administrative Science Quarterly,* 25, 226-251.

Low, M. B. and MacMillan, I. C. (1988). Entrepreneurship: Past research and future challenges. *Journal of Management,* 14: 139-161.

Lumpkin, G. T. and Dess, G. G. (1996). Clarifying the entrepreneurial orientation construct and linking it to performance. *Academy of Management Review,* 21(1), 135–173.

McClelland, D. C. (1961). *The Achieving Society.* Princeton, NJ: Van Nostrand.

McClelland, D. C. (1987). *Human Motivation.* Cambridge, UK: Cambridge University Press.

McDougall, P. P. and Oviatt, B. M. (1997). *International entrepreneurship literature in the 1990s and directions for future research.* In Sexton, D. L. and Smilor, R. W. (eds.), *Entrepreneurship 2000,* 291-320. Chicago: Upstart Publishing.

McGrath, R. G. and MacMillan, I. C. (1992), More like each other than anyone else? A cross-cultural study of entrepreneurial perceptions. *Journal of Business Venturing,* 7(5), 419-429.

McGrath, R. G., MacMillan, I. C., and Scheinberg, S. (1992). Elitists, risk-takers, and rugged individualists? An exploratory analysis of cultural differences between entrepreneurs and non-entrepreneurs. *Journal of Business Venturing*, 7:115-135.

McGrath, R. G., MacMillan, I. C., Yang, E. A., and Tsai, W. (1992). Does culture endure, or is it malleable? Issues for entrepreneurial economic development. *Journal of Business Venturing*, 7(6), 441-458.

Meyer, J. and Rowan, B. (1977). Institutional organizations: Formal structure as myth and ceremony. *American Journal of Sociology*, 83: 340-363.

Meyer, J. W. and Scott, W. R. (1983). *Centralization and the legitimacy problems of local government.* In J.W. Meyer & W.R. Scott (Eds.), *Organizational environments: Ritual and rationality* (pp. 192–215). Beverly Hills, CA: Sage Publications.

Miller, D. (1983). The correlates of entrepreneurship in three types of firms. *Management Science*, 29(7), 770–792.

Mitchell, R. K., Smith, B., Seawright, K. W., and Morse, E. A. (2000). Cross-cultural cognitions and the venture creation decision. *Academy of Management Journal*, 43(5), 974-993.

Morrison, E. W. and Milliken, E. J. (2000). Organizational silence: A barrier to change and development in a pluralistic world. *Academy of Management Review*, 25(4), 706-725.

Mueller, S. L. and Thomas, A. S. (2000). Culture and entrepreneurial potential: A nine country study of locus of control and innovativeness. *Journal of Business Venturing*, 16(1), 51-75.

Mueller, S. L., Thomas, A. S., and Jaeger, A. M. (2002). National entrepreneurial potential: The role of culture, economic development, and political history. *Advances in International Management*, Volume 14: 221-257.

Mulder, M. (1977). *The Daily Power Game*. Leydem, The Netherlands: Martinus Nijhoff.

North, D. C. (1991). Institutions. *Journal of Economic Perspectives*, (1):97–112.

Oviatt, B. and McDougall, P. P. (1994). Toward a theory of international new ventures. *Journal of International Business Studies*, 25: 45-64.

Palich, L. E., and Bagby, D. R. (1995). Using cognitive theory to explain entrepreneurial risk taking: Challenging conventional wisdom. *Journal of Business Venturing*, 10: 425-438.

Parsons, T. (1949). *Essays in Sociological Theory: Theory of Action*. Cambridge, MA: Harvard University Press.

Penrose, E. (1959). *The Theory of the Growth of the Firm*. London: Basil Blackwell & Mott Ltd.

Porac, J. E., Thomas, H., and Baden-Euller, C. (1989). Competitive groups as cognitive communities: The case of Scottish knitwear manufacturers. *Journal of Management Studies,* 26(4), 397-416.

Portes, A. and Sensenbrenner, J. (1993). Embeddedness and immigration: Notes on the social determinants of economic action. *American Journal of Sociology,* 98: 1320- 1350.

Rakos, R. F. (1991). Assertive Behavior: Theory, Research and Training. London: Routledge.

Redding, S. G. (1990). *The Spirit of Chinese Capitalism.* New York, NY: de Gruyter.

Rees, H. and Shah, A. (1986). An empirical analysis of self-employment in the UK. *Journal of Applied Econometrics,* 1, 95–108.

Reynolds, P. D., Camp, S. M., Bygrave, W., Autio, E., and Hay, M. (2001). *Global Entrepreneurship Monitor 2001 Executive Report.* Kansas City, MO: E.M. Kauffman Foundation.

Reynolds, P., Bosma, N., Autio, E., Hunt, S., De Bono, N., Servais, I., Lopez-Garcia, P., and Chin, N. (2005). Global Entrepreneurship Monitor: Data Collection Design and Implementation 1998-2003. *Small Business Economics,* 24(3): 205-231.

Rondinelli, D. A. and Kasarda, J. D. (1992). Foreign trade potential, small enterprise development and job creation in developing countries. *Small Business Economics,* 4: 253-265.

Rotter, J. (1966). Generalized expectancies for internal versus external control of reinforcements. *Psychological Monographs*, 80, Whole No. 609.

Sarasvathy, D. K., Simon, H. A., and Lave, L. (1998). Perceiving and managing business risks: Differences between entrepreneurs and bankers'. *Journal of Economic Behavior and Organization*, 33: 207-226.

Schaffner, J. A. (1993). Rising Incomes and the Shift from Self-Employment to Firm-Based Production. *Economics Letters*, 41, 435–440.

Schriber, J. and Gutek, B. (1987). Some time dimensions of work: Measurement of an underlying aspect of organizational culture. *Journal of Applied Psychology*, 72 (4), 642-650.

Schultz, T.P. (1990). Women's changing participation in the labor force: a world perspective. *Economic Development and Cultural Change*, 38 (3), 457-488.

Schumpeter, J. (1934). *The Theory of Economic Development*. Cambridge, MA: Harvard University Press.

Scott, W. R. (1995). *Institutions and Organizations*. Thousand Oak, CA: Sage.

Scott, W. R. (2005). *Institutional theory: Contributing to a theoretical research program*. In K. G. Smith & M. A. Hitt (eds.), *Great minds in management: The process of theory development*, 460-485. London: Oxford University Press.

Scott, W. R. (2007). *Institutions and organizations: Ideas and interests*. Thousand Oaks, CA: Sage Publications.

Scott, W. R. and Meyer, J. W. (1991). *The rise of training programs in firms and agencies: An institutional perspective*. In L. L. Cummings and B. M. Staw (eds.), *Research in Organizational Behavior*, Vol. 13, pp. 297-326, Greenwich, CT: JAI Press.

Seijts, G. H. (1998). The importance of future time perspective in theories of work motivation. *The Journal of Psychology*, 132 (2), 154-168.

Selznick, P. (1957). *Leadership in Action*. Evanston, IL: Row, Peterson.

Sexton, D. L. and Bowman, N. (1985). The entrepreneur: A capable executive and more. *Journal of Business Venturing*, I(1), 129-140.

Shane, S. (1992). Why do some societies invent more than others?. *Journal of Business Venturing*, 7, 29-46.

Shane, S. (1993). Cultural influences on national rates of innovation. *Journal of Business Venturing*, 8, 59-73.

Shane, S. (1996). Explaining variation in rates of entrepreneurship in the United States: 1899-1988. *Journal of Management*, 22: 747-781.

Shane, S. and Venkataraman, S. (2000). The promise of entrepreneurship as a field of research, *Academy of Management Review*, 25(1): 217-226.

Shapero, A. (1975). The displaced, uncomfortable entrepreneur. *Psychology Today*, 9(6):83-88.

Shapero, A. and Sokol, L. (1982). *The social dimensions of entrepreneurship.* In Kent, C.A., Sexton, D. L., and Vesper, K. H. (eds.). *The Encyclopedia of Entrepreneurship,* Englewood Cliffs, NJ: Prentice-Hall, pp. 72-90.

Sharma, P. and Manikutty, S. (2005). Strategic divestments in family firms: Role of family structure and community culture. *Entrepreneurship Theory and Practice*, 29, 293-311.

Shaw, J. B. (1990). A cognitive categorization model for the study of intercultural management. *Academy of Management Review*, 75(4), 626-645.

Smircich, L. (1983). Concepts of Culture and Organizational Analysis. *Administrative Science Quarterly,* 28(3), 339-358.

Steensma, H. K., Marino, L., Weaver, K. M., and Dickson, P. H. (2000). The influence of national culture on the formation of technology alliances by entrepreneurial firms. *Academy of Management Journal*, 43(5): 951-973.

Stevenson, H. and Jarillo, J. C. (1990). A perspective of Entrepreneurship: Entrepreneurial Management. *Strategic Management Journal.* 11(4), pp. 17-27.

Storey, D. J. (1994). *Understanding the Small Business Sector.* London: Routledge.

Suchman, M. C. (1995). Managing legitimacy: Strategic and institutional approaches. *Academy of Management Review*, 20, 571–610.

Takyi-Asiedu, S. (1993). Some socio-cultural factors retarding entrepreneurial activity in Sub-Saharan Africa. *Journal of Business Venturing*, 8: 91-98.

Teather, E. K. and Chow, C. S. (2000). The geographer and the feng shui practitioner: So close and yet so far apart? *Australian Geographer*, 31(3), 309-332.

Tendam, H. W. (1987). Managerial flexibility: A strategic asset. *Leadership & Organization Development Journal*, 8(2), 11-16.

Thomas, A. S. and Mueller, S. L. (2000). A case for comparative entrepreneurship: Assessing the relevance of culture. *Journal of International Business Studies*, 31:2, 287-301.

Tiessen, J. H. (1997). Individualism, collectivism, and entrepreneurship: A framework for international comparative research. *Journal of Business Venturing*, 12: 367-384.

Triandis, H. C. (1995). *Individualism and Collectivism*. San Francisco, CA: Westview Press.

Trompenaars, F. and Hampden-Turner, C. (1998). *Riding The Waves Of Culture: Understanding Cultural Diversity in Global Business*, (2nd ed.). New York: McGraw-Hill.

van de Vilert, E. and van Yperen, N. (1996). Why cross-national differences in role overload? Don't overlook ambient temperature. *Academy of Management Journal*, 39, 986-1004.

Verheul, I., Wennekers, S., Audretsch, D., and Thurik, R. (2002). *An eclectic theory of entrepreneurship: Policies, institutions and culture*. University of Illinois at Urbana-Champaign's Academy for Entrepreneurial Leadership Historical Research Reference in Entrepreneurship.

Vesper, K. H. (1983). *Entrepreneurship and National Policy*. Chicago, IL: Heller Institute for Small Business Policy Papers.

Ward, J. L. (2000). Reflections on Indian family groups. *Family Business Review*, 13(4), 271–278.

Weber, M. (1904). *From Max Weber: Essays in Sociology*. H.H. Gerth and C. Wright Mills, translated and edited (1948). London: Routledge & Kegan Paul.

Weick, K. E. (1995). *Sensemaking in Organizations*. Thousand Oaks, CA; Sage.

Wildeman, R. E., Hofstede, G., Noorderhaven, N. G., Thurik, A. R., Verhoeven, W. H. J., and Wennekers, A. R. M. (1999). *Self-employment in 23 OECD countries. The role of cultural and economic factors*, Research Report 9811/E, EIM Business and Policy Research, Zoetermeer.

Wortman, M. S., Jr. (1987). Entrepreneurship: An integrating typology and evaluation of the empirical research in the field. *Journal of Management*, 13: 259-279.

Wu, S. (2007). The relationship between national culture and national entrepreneurial activity. *World Review of Entrepreneurship, Management and Sustainable Development*. 3(2):127-141.

Yamada, G. (1996). Urban Informal Employment and Self-Employment in Developing Countries: Theory and Evidence. *Economic Development and Cultural Change* 44, 289–314.

Young, S. A. and Parker, C. P. (1999). Predicting collective climates: Assessing the role of shared work values, needs, employee interaction and work group membership. *Journal of Organizational Behavior*, 20(1), 1199-1218.

Zucker, L. (1977). The role of institutionalization in cultural persistence. *American Sociological Review*, 42:726-743.

9. APPENDICES

APPENDIX A: Definitions of Culture and its Dimensions by GLOBE and Hofstede

	GLOBE
Culture	"Shared motives, values, beliefs, identities, and interpretations or meanings of significant events that result from common experiences of members of collectives that are transmitted across generations"
Performance Orientation	"The degree to which a collective encourages and rewards group members for performance improvement and excellence"
Uncertainty Avoidance	"The extent to which a society, organization, or group relies on social norms, rules, and procedures to alleviate unpredictability of future events"
Institutional Collectivism	"The degree to which organizational and societal institutional practices encourage and reward collective distribution of resources and collective action"
In-Group Collectivism	"The degree to which individuals express pride, loyalty, and cohesiveness in their organizations and families"
Assertiveness	"The degree to which individuals are assertive, confrontational, and aggressive in their relationships with others"
Future Orientation	"The extent to which individuals engage in future-oriented behaviors such as delaying gratification, planning, and investing in the future"
Power Distance	"The degree to which members of an organization or society expect and agree that power should be unequally shared"

Gender Egalitarianism	"The degree to which a collective minimizes gender inequality"
Humane Orientation	"The degree to which a collective encourages and rewards individuals for being fair, altruistic, generous, caring, and kind to others"

Hofstede	
Culture	"Set of shared values, beliefs, and expected behaviors" OR "The collective programming of the mind that distinguishes the members of one group or category of people from another"
Power Distance	"The extent to which the less powerful members of institutions and organizations within a country expect and accept that power is distributed unequally"
Uncertainty Avoidance	"The extent to which the members of a culture feel threatened by uncertain or unknown situations"
Individualism-Collectivism	"Individualism stands for a society in which the ties between individuals are loose: Everyone is expected to look after him/herself and her/his immediate family only" AND "Collectivism stands for a society in which people from birth onwards are integrated into strong, cohesive in-groups, which throughout people's lifetime continue to protect them in exchange for unquestioning loyalty"
Masculinity-Femininity	"Masculinity stands for a society in which social gender roles are clearly distinct: Men are supposed to be assertive, tough, and focused on material success; women are supposed to be more modest, tender, and concerned with the quality of life" AND "Femininity stands for a society in which social gender roles overlap: Both men and women are supposed to be modest, tender, and concerned with the quality of life"
Long vs. Short Term Orientation (or Confucian Dynamism)	"Long Term Orientation stands for the fostering of virtues oriented towards future rewards, in particular, perseverance and thrift" AND "Short Term Orientation stands for the fostering of virtues related to the past and present, in particular, respect for tradition, preservation of 'face' and fulfilling social obligations"

APPENDIX B: Literature Review of Relevant Empirical Studies

Paper	Research Questions	Measures of National Culture	Data Source	Sample	Major Findings
Shane (1992)	What is the association between national culture and national rates of innovation?	Individualism, Power Distance	**Culture:** Hofstede. **Innovation:** Per capita *patent filings.*	33 countries	National rates of innovation are positively correlated with individualism and negatively with power distance.
Shane (1993)	What effect does national culture have on national rates of innovation?	Individualism, Power Distance, Uncertainty Avoidance, and Masculinity	**Culture:** Hofstede. **Innovation:** Per capita *number of trademarks.*	33 countries	National rates of innovation are positively correlated with individualism and negatively correlated with uncertainty avoidance and power distance. Masculinity had no significant correlation.
Davidsson (1995)	What is the interaction among structural characteristics, culture, beliefs concerning entrepreneurship, and entrepreneurial intentions?	**The Entrepreneurial Values Index:** Achievement Motivation, Locus of Control, Need for Autonomy, and Change Orientation. **The Entrepreneurial Beliefs:** Societal contribution, financial payoff, perceived risk, social status.	**Values & Beliefs:** Constructed survey. **Entrepreneurship:** New firm formation rates.	2,200 individuals within Sweden	Scores on the Entrepreneurial Values index have correlated with regional rates of new firm formation within Sweden. No support for the Beliefs.

Study	Research Question	Concepts	Sample	Findings
Davidsson & Wiklund (1997)	Controlling for economic/structural factors, is culture associated with differences in rates of new-firm formation?	**Values:** Change orientation, need for achievement, need for autonomy, Jante-mentality competitiveness. **Beliefs:** Societal contribution, financial payoff, perceived risk, social status, workload, know-how.	**Values & Beliefs:** Constructed survey. **Entrepreneurship:** New firm formation rates. 1,313 individuals within Sweden	Cultural values and beliefs have a small but statistically significant association with regional rates of new-firm formation within Sweden.
Begley & Tan (2001)	Do cultural values play a role in the desire and perception of feasibility of new businesses? Do East Asian and Anglo Saxon countries differ in the score and impact of such cultural values on entrepreneurship?	Social status of entrepreneurship, shame from business failure (losing face), culture's value of innovation, culture's value of work.	Own-developed scales to measure 1) the proposed cultural concepts and **2)** the "Desirability" and "Feasibility" of starting a business (intentions). 1,253 MBA students in 10 countries (six East Asian and four Anglo Saxon)	Social status of entrepreneurship positively predicts both Feasibility and Desirability, while value of innovation negatively predicts both. Both shame of failure and societal value of work negatively predict Feasibility. Social status will positively predict interest in entrepreneurship better in East Asia than the West. Shame of business failure will partially negatively predict interest in entrepreneurship better in East Asia than the West.

126

	Research Question	Culture Dimensions	Entrepreneurship / Sample	Findings
				Value of Innovation negatively predicted Feasibility among East Asians and Desirability among Anglos. In East Asia, as societal value of work increased, Feasibility decreased.
Wu (2007)	Given the limited empirical studies, are national entrepreneurial activity and Hofstede's national culture related? And how are they related?	Individualism, Power Distance, Uncertainty Avoidance, and Masculinity	**Culture:** Hofstede. **Entrepreneurship:** GEM's TEA and FEA 34 countries	No support for all hypotheses - except Individualism, which was found to be negatively related to TEA (opposite of hypothesis).
Mueller, Thomas, & Jaeger (2002)	How do culture, economic development, and political history play a role in the potential venture creation (individual entrepreneurship orientation) across countries?	Individualism, Power Distance, Uncertainty Avoidance, and Masculinity	**Culture:** Hofstede. **Potential Entrepreneurship:** Self-constructed measure of Individual EO (locus of control & innovativeness) 2,700 under-graduate students in 17 countries	No support for all relevant hypotheses - except Masculinity, which was positively related with the propensity for engaging in entrepreneurial activities among students.

www.ingramcontent.com/pod-product-compliance
Lightning Source LLC
Chambersburg PA
CBHW021957170526
45157CB00003B/1037